SHORTCUT 8
170 DOCTOR QUOTES

by LINKED IN AND TOWN HALL ACHIEVER OF THE YEAR
BY NOMINEE ENTREPRENEUR OF THE YEAR
GRAND HOMAGE LV'S DIVERSITY
WORLD TOP100 DOCTORS

Dr BAK NGUYEN, DMD

TO ALL THOSE LOOKING TO WALK THEIR DESTINY AND
WONDERING WHY THEY FEEL SO DIFFERENT.

by Dr BAK NGUYEN

ISBN: 978-1-989536-82-7

Published by: Dr. BAK PUBLISHING COMPANY
Dr.BAK 0100

DISCLAIMER

« The general information, opinions and advice contained in this medium and/or the books, audiobooks, podcasts and publications on Dr. Bak Nguyen's (legal name Dr. Ba Khoa Nguyen) website or social media (hereinafter the "Opinions") present general information on various topics. The Opinions are intended for informational purposes only.

No information contained in the Opinions is a substitute for an expert, consultation, advice, diagnosis or professional treatment. No information contained in the Opinions is a substitute for professional advice and should not be construed as consultation or advice.

Nothing in the Opinions should be construed as professional advice related to the practice of dentistry, medical advice or any other form of advice, including legal or financial advice, professional opinion, care or diagnosis, but strictly as general information. All information from the Opinions is for informational purposes only.

Any user who disagrees with the terms of this Disclaimer should immediately cease using or referring to the Opinions. Any action by the user in connection with the information contained in the Opinions is solely at the user's discretion.

The general information contained in the Opinions is provided "as is" and without warranty of any kind, either expressed or implied. Dr. Bak Nguyen (legal name Dr. Ba Khoa Nguyen) makes every effort to ensure that the information is complete and accurate. However, there is no guarantee that the general information contained in the Opinions is always available, truthful, complete, up-to-date or relevant.

The Opinions expressed by Dr. Bak Nguyen (legal name Dr. Ba Khoa Nguyen) are personal and expressed in his own name and do not reflect the opinions of his companies, partners and other affiliates.

Dr. Bak Nguyen (legal name Dr. Ba Khoa Nguyen) also disclaims any responsibility for the content of any hyperlinks included in the Opinions.

Always seek the advice of your expert advisors, physicians or other qualified professionals with any questions you may have regarding your condition. Never disregard professional advice or delay in seeking it because of something you have read, seen or heard in the Opinions. »

ABOUT THE AUTHOR

From Canada, **Dr. BAK NGUYEN**, Nominee Ernst and Young Entrepreneur of the year, Grand Homage Lys DIVERSITY, LinkedIn & TownHall Achiever of the year and TOP 100 Doctors 2021. Dr Bak is a cosmetic dentist, CEO and founder of Mdex & Co. His company is revolutionizing the dental field. Speaker and motivator, he wrote 72 books over 36 months accumulating many world records (to be officialized). His books are covering:

- **ENTREPRENEURSHIP**
- **LEADERSHIP**
- **QUEST OF IDENTITY**
- **DENTISTRY AND MEDICINE**
- **PARENTING**
- **CHILDREN'S BOOKS**
- **PHILOSOPHY**

In 2003, he founded Mdex, a dental company upon which in 2018, he launched the most ambitious private endeavour to reform the dental industry, Canada wide. Philosopher, he has close to his heart the quest of happiness of the people surrounding him, patients and colleagues alike. In 2020, he launched an International collaborative initiative named **THE ALPHAS** to share knowledge and for Entrepreneurs and Doctors to thrive through the Greatest Pandemic and Economic depression of our time.

In 2016, he co-found with Tranie Vo, Emotive World Incorporated, a tech research company to use technology to empower happiness and sharing. U.A.X. the ultimate audio experience is the landmark project on which the team is advancing, utilizing the technics of the movie industry and the advancement in ARTIFICIAL INTELLIGENCE to save the book industry and to upgrade the continuing education space.

These projects have allowed Dr Nguyen to attract interests from the international and diplomatic community and he is now the centre of a global discussion in the wellbeing and the future of the health profession. It is in that matter that he shares his thoughts and encourages the health community to share their own stories.

"It's not worth it go through it alone! Together, we stand, alone, we fall."

Motivational speaker and serial entrepreneur, philosopher and author, from his own words, Dr Nguyen describes himself as a dentist by circumstances, an entrepreneur by nature and a communicator by passion.

He also holds recognitions from the Canadian Parliament and the Canadian Senate.

170 DOCTOR QUOTES

by Dr BAK NGUYEN

INTRODUCTION
BY Dr BAK NGUYEN

INTRODUCTION
by Dr. BAK NGUYEN

This is the last and 8th volume of the **SHORTCUT series**. What started as a cheat revealed to be the biggest undertaking of my author career. With months in research, prep work, and sorting.

How foolish was I, thinking that it would be an easy copy-paste ride? To revisit each of my books, each of my quotes, to sort them out into categories, and to organize these same categories into a new narrative, was nothing of a cheat.

To write book 1 and 2, that's fun! To write a trilogy, that's empowering, inspiring. But to write, on my own, a **DRAGON series** (8 books), that's no joke! Actually, now that I am at the last volume, I will say how proud I am.

I found a way to revamp reading and to empower the **Personal Quest of Identity** and the **Rise of each into their Legend**. These 100 books of mine are all dedicated to our personal evolution and to find power, ease, and speed to keep rising. That's my legacy.

This morning I woke up on the great news that **SHORTCUT volume 7 - Happiness** is now available in paperback version on Amazon. We are Monday morning. I started that book last Saturday and submitted the manuscript Sunday around noon, yesterday.

Not only the complete writing of that book was done in 24 hours, the editing in 2 hours; 90 minutes after its submission to Amazon, it was available worldwide on Kindle, on a Sunday afternoon. Can you think of a better way to start your week?

That was yesterday. Today, more good news as the paperback, the biggest of the release, is live worldwide and official, I will be welcoming its arrival on Apple Books within the next hours and Barnes and Noble, may be tomorrow.

These **big 3** are my biggest fans and my support system. I told you to reach your checkpoints and to jump from win to win to keep up your momentum. Well, these 3 alone will provide me with 4 wins per book. That's part of my recipe to replenish and to keep pushing, accelerating.

The last volume was about **HAPPINESS**, a huge contrast with the previous volume, the dark volume of **POWER**. On that one, I changed my morning routine a little bit. After the exhaustion of volume 6 - **POWER**, which took 6 days to complete, I took a full day to edit and publish.

Then, I decided to take the rest of that day, slow. I went on to finish the preparation work of the last 2 books I have to write before completing my landmark record of 100 books.

By prep work, I meant, making the covers, preparing the template, table of contents, and the copy-paste of the quotes and the formatting. The only thing that I will have to do when I will be ready, is to start writing the introduction and to follow the flow.

Before going to bed that night, I also updated Dr. Bak's website and books library. Pushing the updates online and releasing them on social media were also part of my routine, especially since I am running for the 2 landmark world records of **96 books written within 48 months** and, 2 weeks later, **100 books within 4 years**.

Keeping my audience posted about my days and progress has been part of my routine and support system. When you write as much, as fast, and that you are basically alone with your words, the whole secret is to keep your energy and motivation.

The answer is **YES** and the timing is **NOW**. That is what I learnt from my miles running from momentum to momentum. And my hormones? I know all too well how those are essential ingredients to my success, my momentum.

If the last volume took 6 days, I was running low on hormones and feelings. Discipline and willpower carried me to the finished line. There was no style nor ease there. It was pain and fatigue. I was even too tired to celebrate a win!

My odds went from 4.5 days per book down to 3.33 days per book before reaching out of *real estate* to complete my 100 books within 4 years. That is 18 hours per book that I just lost!

Nonetheless, I took it slow, by my pace. I took a day working on prep work and setting up the last 3 books to write before 100. **SHORTCUT volume 6 - HAPPINESS, SHORTCUT volume 7 - DOCTOR**, and **HOW TO BOOST YOUR CREATIVITY TO NEW HEIGHTS** are the last miles before the finished line.

Saturday morning, I woke up, and instead of going to my desk and laptop, I went for the piano instead. I played, for a few hours. I enjoyed improvising. I even got William to join too. Actually, I kind of forced him. I showed him the basics and set him up to play with the chords.

Well, within 10 minutes, he was playing along with THE SCORE, his favourite band (playing from YouTube). I showed him how to read the chords and where they were on the piano. We both enjoy that magical moment as he amazed both himself and me!

That lasted for the time of 3 songs, maybe 4. Listening to him playing, I was transported as a proud father. I just taught my son the power of music and how to learn to play on the fly. Before then, he never played that song! By the fourth time, his friends showed up.

He and his friends were going to the water pack with Tranie and her friends. I kissed them goodbye. Here I was, alone in the mansion with a beautiful whole free day in front of me. I sat at my desk and started writing.

I took a few breaks. I went to the pool once and stopped to have lunch around 4 PM. I was enjoying the flow of time and the sun. I was compelled to go back and to keep writing. I wasn't pushing, I was flowing. They return around 9 PM. I was at my last chapter to write, you know the biggest one in the **SHORTCUT series**, the chapter about the "power of quotes".

I sat down with Tranie and William and sharing with them their anecdotes of both, their great day and mine. Then, I went back to finish my chapter. Before 12 AM, I was done. I just went straight to bed. I will be correcting and revising tomorrow. And that is how I managed to complete a book within 24 hours, including the 8 I spent sleeping!

By the next morning, I spent 90 minutes revising and started the publishing process. By the beginning of the afternoon, people could read it on Kindle.

The writing of that last volume was flawless and went like a breeze, just like William learning to play piano yesterday morning! I took the rest of the day to spend family time with Tranie, William, and my parents. Now, everyone was joining in my excitement and celebrations, even my parents!

I had much to celebrate. With the completion of volume 7, I only had 2 books left to write before my landmark world record. That also put me back at the odds of 4 days per book, with 8 days left. I basically just gain 8 hours per book!

But much more, I just graduated you and me, from the **SHORTCUT** journey. If the franchise has 8 volumes, the first

7 are for the general public. Volume 8, **DOCTOR** is a special one, it is kind of a Steve Job's "Oh, one last thing…"

And this is my "Oh, one last thing" volume. This one is to honour the legacy that I have received as a member of the medical elite, as a doctor. This is what I keep from my 25 years in the medical ranks since my first days in dental school to my rise as one of the **world's TOP 100 doctors** of 2021.

"Doctors too, will have to heal."
Dr. Bak Nguyen

That's quote #2521. Being one of you, for a quarter of a century, I am now shifting my attention from my patients and my audience to you, dear colleagues, doctors, and white coats. This won't be my first time taking healing and personal growth to our ranks.

Writing the **SHORTCUT series** gave me the opportunity to revisit and make sense of the process and the mapping to heal and to rise. Well, we, white coats, are giving our best day after day, not having the right for any mistake. That's the trade of champions. Well, that is called average within our ranks.

We spend our lives healing and putting the needs of others before our own. That is what heroes do. We do it on a daily basis, we called it average. And to do it with minimum recognition because we are bound to humility and professional secrecy, what do we have to replenish with?

Do you think that I am exaggerating? Well, I was giving that speech 3 years ago. I needed to dig to find personal examples that would rally everyone. Well, today in the midst of the COVID war, how are we treating our health professionals, the white coats, doctors, nurses, and team members who are healing the world?

At the beginning of the COVID war, we were heroes as we held the frontline of the war against COVID. 15 months later, after we've been exhausted on the frontline giving it our best, our all, how do we get thanked?

We are submitted to the law of silence, to disciplinary hearing if we do not keep standing in line with an improvising leadership, and even worst: as the vaccination campaign is gaining ground, we've been stripped from our rights to choose, forced to be vaccinated to keep practicing.

"Last year heroes for keeping the frontline without a vaccine. This year, fired if we do not take the vaccine!"

Don't get me wrong, I am not anti-vaccine. Myself, I received both doses, out of respect for my patients and by solidarity to my wife, Tranie. I even wrote a book with William at the beginning of this year to explain what is a vaccine from a science standpoint: **THE VACCINE, A TALE OF SPIES AND ALIENS**. Yup, we wrote that one for kids and their parents. So no, I am not anti-vaccine.

That said, I am sharing the pain and disgust of our ungratefulness to our heroes. How do you heal from that? And this is my mission, within this journey with you, white coats. I won't be wasting your time and mind blaming those in power. If you want change, run for office!

I might, if things keep getting worse. In the meantime, let's take care of one another. You are champions and heroes. You are humble and dedicated. Thank you. How about that for a starter? Thank you and you are worth it!

More than that, COVID has shown us that no one is immune to fatigue, burn-out, and exhaustion. Dealing with urgencies all the time, not having the right for

21

mistakes, and to uphold the highest standards always and always, we too, have the right to heal.

So, it is okay not to be perfect. You might not have the right to fail, but you still need to cope! If you don't, you will be making a fatal mistake because you were running for too long on your **wearing off**. Don't do that to yourself, the world needs you, all of you, white coats.

We too have the right to heal, to grow, and to find our voice. I am one of you. I found my healing, my growth, and finally, my voice.

I am Dr. Bak and I am one of you. I am not better than any of you. If anything, I was just more sensitive to the human aspect of healing since the beginning of my medical training and journey. As I am helping the rest of the world to heal and to found their powers, I will help you too to heal.

You are already powerful and you are helping others to heal, that's your function and passion. Since growth occurs at the giving end, how come we are still looking for ours? Well, we have to heal first, before we can grow.

As white coats, we have been trained to grow, to be humble, and to keep helping. What is often the obstacle is the denial that we too, need to cope. Not coping daily will cause wounds that we will need to heal from. And just like any of the wounds, unattended wounds will get worse and cause complications.

Why is it that depression, burn-out, and even suicide are common themes within our numbers? Because we are in denial until we run out of time and space. And even when we are opening up, we must isolate ourselves and hide from the shame of needing help. This is wrong! That's what Conformity pushed us to.

Well, the mission of this journey is not to lecture society and our institution on how to treat its assets. Let's do what no one seems to do, let's take care of one another and heal first. Then, we can get back at healing the world and, maybe, even the broken institutions of our society. People first, the institutions after!

For our journey ahead, this is my mission with you, to help you cope and heal, with grace, with honour, with dignity, with gratitude. We swore to do no harm, let's now taste our own medicine. We too are humans!

This is **Shortcut volume 8, Doctor**. Welcome to the Alphas.

Remember, you treat the present and the future, not the past.

Dr. BAK NGUYEN

PART 1
"DOCTOR"
by Dr. BAK NGUYEN

Doctor, that is a title that some of us worked hard, day and night, for. Doctor has been for some, like me, the life goal of a past legacy, the passport into the elite, the fallen dreams of those who love us. For others, doctor is a life mission and the license to do good.

Well, doctor is all of the above. And that's how I would like to start this chapter with, doctor is not a status but a state of mind. Much more that a goal, a function, or simply nobility, doctor is a state of mind with much history, dreams, and drama.

This is from the giving end. On the receiving end, we do not treat illnesses, accidents, and handicaps, but humans with histories, dreams, and drama. And this is the essence of this journey together, as doctors, as white coats.

"Be human to heal humans."
Dr. Bak Nguyen

That's quote #2522. I would first apologize, even if I use doctor to address to you, this journey is not exclusive to those with the DR, letters of nobility, before their names but to all of us who are wearing a white coat, a scrub, and who are putting all that we are on the table to help the next person coming in.

"As such, DR is a status, white coat is a function, and to be successful, it has to become a state of mind."
Dr. Bak Nguyen

That's quote #2523. I could go on and on about the powers I discovered as a white coat. I will simply say as much. The nobility of being a doctor, of putting your interest before mine, elevated my thinking and comprehension to the next level, one above resistance. This is how I realized that "the only way to grow is by sharing..." and "growth occurs at the giving end" (years later).

Well, those are the reasons why I kept the designation of DR in front of my name, as I reinvented myself, from Dr. Nguyen to Dr. Bak. It was to keep the reminder that I had to put your interests before mine.

Well, that philosophy brought me the respect and favour of the financial world. In their views, I have clearly defined a market to serve and I am dedicated to bring it to the next level. They love the words market and define. As for me, I was genuine.

As an author, I went from writing my first book to become a multiple world records pretender, just because I wanted to share more, to more and with more. More people, more subjects, more adventures, this was my way to abundance, always from the giving end..

I elevated myself, doing more in the last 4 years than in my first 40 because I encountered less resistance, starting with myself, my judgment, and pride. As soon as I put your interest before mine, everything shifted.

Prior to that, I was ready, I healed and I was whole. I went through the healing process first. That process was mainly about cutting down the denials, the lies, and the blind angles. The first lie that I dropped was about perfection.

"Perfection is a lie."
Dr. Bak Nguyen

From that point, I built up my Confidence and my voice. Confidence, not arrogance. I am still not sure of how to point you a definitive difference between the both of them without stepping into the realm of opinions. Nonetheless, I can clearly tell you how to avoid the question completely: by putting the interests of others before your own!

If you serve, arrogance is not even remotely close to the table. Jealousy might be, but not arrogance. And jealousy, with its ugly head, is obvious, it is an easy guest to identify and define.

So to keep yourself away from arrogance, serve! Isn't that what we do, on a daily basis, white coats? If I told you that most of my powers are originated from serving others, you have access to the same **Oasis of powers**.

"To find, touch and even yield these powers,
you just need to heal first, white coats!"
Dr. Bak Nguyen

That's quote #2524. And this is the hope that I am sharing with you. This is the promise that I am putting on the table, clearly and without ambiguity. You all have the **lion heart** to grow and to find your power to serve more, to serve better.

What is keeping you from such powers is often your mind and the way you see the world. Worst, the way you see yourself. I know that song all too well, letting others to define me…

Can you judge me? Can I judge you? This is a sad side effect of our elite medical training and selection process, we compare and we judge. Then, to keep things as predictable as possible, we studied and applied protocols, recipes. To clearly identify our targets, we stopped talking about people but about viruses, proteins, and antibodies.

We've been so good at keeping the emotions and the human part from the equation that we forgot about the human, its complexity, and its power. No, this is not an opinion.

Even in fundamental medicine, we have to bow down to the spirit and the mind as we accepted the placebo effect, of people healing as they are believing. Well, we might have accepted that one but we made it into a boundary, a liability, never have we seen it as an asset.

Our views, the way we treat our patients mirrored on us, day in and day out, day after day. As much as we

dehumanized medicine, we dehumanized ourselves too in the process. Who does not have the right to be tired? We don't, as white coats. Who does not make mistake? We don't, as white coats. Who does not have the right to be sick? Well, we do and feel shame for it...

Even our science and art have broken us, at our core. Science is built on methodology, hypothesis, and experimentation (trial and error). The basis of science is to have a hypothesis, to follow a methodology, and to readjust to the outcome.

Well, medicine is science. We diagnose (hypothesis), we plan our treatment (methodology) and the outcome should always be perfect healing, at least, this is the standard of expectation. What happened to the **readjustment phase** which is the most important act in science? Well, we cut that out of the process. Instead, if we fail, we have to stand on trial and defend each one of our actions.

I do understand the importance of the *no mistake* in medicine, trust me, I do. But since we have cut out a major part of the scientific methodology, what did we find to replace it with? Nothing!

Our profession coped by imposing more continuous education, protocols, and methodology at the first 2 phases of science, diagnostic and treatment plans… and nothing at the reevaluation and adjustment phase. Well, in science, that is where the growth and comprehension occur.

So on, that, we are no scientists. Make your peace with it. We are glorified workers, operators. This is mainly what we are. This comes and leaves even a bigger hole in our esteem.

Were we not the elite? We are asked to perform as champions since our first days, people expect the best from us, day in and day out, without much break, as what we are is a glorified worker?

What about our passion to give again and again, daily, putting the interest of others before our own? Isn't that why heroes are recognized for? We do it, do not receive much praises from it, and yet, we believe in it as our primal core directive. And we are just glorified workers?

Well, if we were anything more, would our governments and management treated us so badly, ordering us around in time of crisis, discarding us at will to fit their narrative, from heroes to be fired? How do you explain that we put all of the dental elite of the world on pause all at once without blinking twice in the 3 first months of COVID)?

We did that because the world was in shortage of medical equipment. Do you still think that you are the elite, my dear dentist colleagues? And the physicians, where is your liberty, wisdom, and science came into play as *management* required your hands and time and skills while imposing you the law of silence?

We are nothing but glorified workers. There is nothing wrong with being a worker. What is damaging are the denial and the lies. We are not scientists nor elite. That said, we have been trained as elite and we are forged as such.

Leave the complaints and the retributions behind, those will only lead to more denial, pride, and pain. Instead, why don't you allow yourself to heal first, to cope with the void, and to grow.

I told you that white coats all have the heart to do so. If not, you won't have last that long. You are kind and generous. Now, be kind and generous with yourself. Drop the denial and start healing. That's healing.

Then, about growth, I told you time and time again that growth occurs at the giving end. Isn't it what we do every day? We just need to put the right mindset in place, we were trained to succeed in such conditions.

Then, to keep growing and to rise, discipline will be required. Discipline and curiosity. Well, how did we earned our titles and credentials? From discipline and the belief that we are scientists (curiosity). If anything, the medical selection process proved that right with each of us. This should boost your confidence!

In short, we have all the ingredients to rise and to keep growing, making the world a better place. So why not do so? What you do with your powers and your life is your choice. My goal here was to show you that the is a choice. There is so much more than what we have been shown in our training.

I am not a victim. I won't complain about my training and choices. Now that I am a white coat, I will leverage that training to rise and to raise the average with me. No more comparison, no more beating the average, no more lies.

I am rising because I serve the average, because I raise the average. That's leadership! The beauty of it is that I do not have to choose between who I was and who I am. I am one and the same, only now, I see clearly what is what, and I leverage everything in my favour, serving the world.

Drop the lies, denials, and pride and acknowledge how good it feels. Drop the past and feel how powerful you are. If writing, I found much proximity with anyone looking to heal, well, I must say that in you, white coats, I have even greater hopes. Hopes, not expectations.

Since you have been trained to perform and to overcome all the obstacles, and with a heart like yours, imagine the differences you will be bringing to our world with great powers. You know how, I just need to show you where to look!

With great respect and humility, I thank all of you for your continuous service and dedication. To you, doctors, white coats, here is the **ODE OF THE WHITE COATS**.

We gave it our best every day
We gave it our all until nothing is left in the grey
We do it again and again until we break
And that's our only mistake.

We are champions
And yet, in our ranks, that's average

Hope and healing are our beacons
And still, our hope is in shortage
Because we wear white coats

You call us doctors
Trusting us with your lives, hopes, and pains
With our science and skills, we will leave no quarters
That's the promise, the blood in our veins

We are heroes
Daily and always ready to restore
We stand tall chasing away pain and shadows
We give and give until we have no more
We are white coats

We bow to science, proof, and facts
And still, even in Science, nothing is ever exact
So forget perfection, which is a lie
Understand Harmony to not die

To treat, we balanced the faulty
To heal, we need to act swiftly and gently
Not just with others but with ourselves too
That's the only way to keep be useful to you

We bear the world on our shoulders
We are healers, not soldiers
It's ok to feel drained, It's fine to be tired
Even if complaining isn't our standard

We are white coats
To keep rolling the stone uphill
We too, need healing and hopes
And once recharged, nothing withstand our will

We are white Coats
We are powerful because with we are serving
Giving and Healing, first arrived and last leaving

Because we are white Coats.

We are champions
And yet, in our ranks, that's average
We are heroes
We stand tall chasing away pain and shadows
We need each other to heal, to grow
Because we are white Coats.

This is **Shortcut volume 8, Doctor**. Welcome to the Alphas.

Remember, you treat the present and the future, not the past

Dr. BAK NGUYEN

PART 2

"93 DOCTOR QUOTES"

by Dr. BAK NGUYEN

2264

"If we are measured by the size of our heart,
we are in heavy league!"

Dr. Bak Nguyen

2265

"We are giving our best, day after day,
with no chance for failure. In anything that I know,
this is called a champion. We, we call it average!"

Dr. Bak Nguyen

2266

"In our ranks, elite is average and humility
and standard. But we are still humans!"

Dr. Bak Nguyen

2267

"We treat people, not teeth."

Dr. Bak Nguyen

2268

"To be happy, you must be human."

Dr. Bak Nguyen

2269

"From the top down, from the desire to what is next, make it a straight story!"

Dr. Bak Nguyen

2270

"White coats, happiness is a result of our work and by extension, we are our work, thus, we are Happiness!"

Dr. Bak Nguyen

2271

"We are not simply happy because we have healed the world! The world heals from our happiness! And so on, and so on!"

Dr. Bak Nguyen

2272

FROM PROFESSION HEALTH

"Remember, you treat the present and the future, not the past."

Dr. Bak Nguyen

2273

FROM PROFESSION HEALTH

"Do not discard hope from your treatment plan."

Dr. Bak Nguyen

2274

FROM PROFESSION HEALTH

"We are white coats, half science, half human."

Dr. Bak Nguyen

2275

FROM PROFESSION HEALTH

"Our training, our nature, will always push us to learn and adapt along the way. For as long as we'll do, we'll learn."

Dr. Bak Nguyen

2276
FROM PROFESSION HEALTH
"Be whole and be happy and you will have transcended your white coat!"
Dr. Bak Nguyen

2277
FROM PROFESSION HEALTH
"Just like being whole and selfless, you'll borrow the will of someone else and the patient, this time, is you."
Dr. Bak Nguyen

2278
FROM PROFESSION HEALTH
"The efficiency of science was saving us from our own devils. So we went on, carrying both the shadow and armour derived from it on our shoulders."
Dr. Bak Nguyen

2279
FROM PROFESSION HEALTH
"Inspire your team, inspire your patient, inspire your rise!"
Dr. Bak Nguyen

2280

"We are in a fight against the odds,
not against each other!"

Dr. Bak Nguyen

2281

"We are all in it together!"

Dr. Bak Nguyen

2282

"Heal yourself to heal the world!"

Dr. Bak Nguyen

2283

"We have nothing to prove!
We are and do!
Passion, hope and love!
We are white coats!"

Dr. Bak Nguyen

2284

"We are glorified workers."

Dr. Bak Nguyen

2285

"Finances is both mathematics and psychology,
just like medicine is half science half human."

Dr. Bak Nguyen

2286

"Finance works the other way around,
desire outcome - diagnostic - course of actions."

Dr. Bak Nguyen

2287

"There is no glass anymore to see the nobility
of our commitment and, at the same time,
our faces from the reflection."

Dr. Bak Nguyen

2288
FROM PROFESSION HEALTH
"Our psychological training process started even before we received our admission letter."
Dr. Bak Nguyen

2289
FROM INDUSTRIES' DISRUPTORS
"We keep our dentists happy so they, in turn, can keep their patients happy."
Dr. Bak Nguyen

2290
FROM INDUSTRIES' DISRUPTORS
"Every time I put on a white coat, it wasn't me that was important, it was my patient!"
Dr. Bak Nguyen

2291
FROM HOW TO NOT FAIL AS A DENTIST
"The first rule of professional intelligence is never to leave your ground."
Dr. Bak Nguyen

2292

"In medicine, just like most in life,
doubt is a poison that you do not need."

Dr. Bak Nguyen

2293

"The first role of a dentist is to identify and educate.
We should add to comfort to that list."

Dr. Bak Nguyen

2294

"Keep your integrity, be kind and care!
That's why they are calling you doctor."

Dr. Bak Nguyen

2295

"Embrace the facts and transform
your liability into responsibility."

Dr. Bak Nguyen

2296

"I succeeded as a dentist
because I put my pride aside."

Dr. Bak Nguyen

2297

"I am not a doctor. My function when I serve
is as a doctor. I am human, just like them."

Dr. Bak Nguyen

2298

"Give to your patients what they need.
Sometimes, it is not what they want."

Dr. Bak Nguyen

2299

"The title and the white coat are about a function,
not an identity."

Dr. Bak Nguyen

2300

"In my book, to consent to a treatment is to trust."

Dr. Bak Nguyen

2301

"A patient is a whole with teeth, body, health and emotions. Even if we only have a licence to treat the teeth, our title as doctors obliges us to see the whole."

Dr. Bak Nguyen

2302

"Respect everyone as you want to be treated."

Dr. Bak Nguyen

2303

"Our structures must remain at a human level to allow people to relate. To relate and to establish a trust."

Dr. Bak Nguyen

2304

"There is a fundamental difference between building a practice and a business."

Dr. Bak Nguyen

2305
FROM SUCCESS IS A CHOICE
"We are doctors, but we are not above money,
just like no one is above the law."
Dr. Bak Nguyen

2306
FROM SUCCESS IS A CHOICE
"Your only regret should be the same of my patients,
why haven't you done it sooner?"
Dr. Bak Nguyen

2307
FROM RELEVANCY
"The last I checked, medicine is a science, not an art!"
Dr. Bak Nguyen

2308
FROM RELEVANCY
"I succeeded as a dentist because my patients
gave me purpose and the need
to perfect my skills and craft."
Dr. Bak Nguyen

2309

"COVID-19 showed us how vulnerable
we really are, with 3% relevancy or less!"

Dr. Bak Nguyen

2310

FROM RELEVANCY

"As a cosmetic dentist, I learnt to listen to my patients
and stopped locking down on them,
telling them what they need."

Dr. Bak Nguyen

2311

FROM MIDAS TOUCH

"Caught between technological advancements and
COVID-19, our TOUCH will keep our relevancy."

Dr. Bak Nguyen

2312

FROM MIDAS TOUCH

"The hunger is good and you will need to fuel
yourself before going out there and
start giving again!"

Dr. Bak Nguyen

2313
FROM MIDAS TOUCH
"Talk to be understood, not to express."
Dr. Bak Nguyen

2314
FROM MIDAS TOUCH
"We are in power, we are in authority.
The power to deliver and the authority to serve,
nothing more, and nothing less."
Dr. Bak Nguyen

2315
FROM MIDAS TOUCH
"We are white coats, we stand for excellence,
for knowledge, for them. What is it to be shy about?"
Dr. Bak Nguyen

2316
FROM MIDAS TOUCH
"Renew your trust in yourself and in people, so age
will become wisdom; expertise, nature, and
empowerment. This is a promise."
Dr. Bak Nguyen

2317

FROM MIDAS TOUCH

"People don't like to be there,
that's the truth, and your way in!"

Dr. Bak Nguyen

2318

FROM MIDAS TOUCH

"You can't change their expectations,
but you can change their experience."

Dr. Bak Nguyen

2319

FROM MIDAS TOUCH

"A smile will go a long way."

Dr. Bak Nguyen

2320

FROM MIDAS TOUCH

"I just needed to listen, identify the need, and
reformulate theirs words into steps of medicine."

Dr. Bak Nguyen

2321

FROM MIDAS TOUCH

"A white coat is 50% science and 50% human."

Dr. Bak Nguyen

2322

FROM MIDAS TOUCH

"Give them your heart,
you will have their trust in return."

Dr. Bak Nguyen

2323

FROM MIDAS TOUCH

"Give them what they need. Tell them what to feed.
Make them feel warm and neat."

Dr. Bak Nguyen

2324

FROM MIDAS TOUCH

"Humility is to know that we are there to care and to
serve. Confidence is the faith that we have in them,
in our hard hammered sciences and in ourselves."

Dr. Bak Nguyen

2325

FROM MIDAS TOUCH

"You are more powerful than you think!"

Dr. Bak Nguyen

2326
FROM MIDAS TOUCH
"As a white coat, be open and stand your ground."
Dr. Bak Nguyen

2327
FROM MIDAS TOUCH
"Be a problem solver and reverse engineer."
Dr. Bak Nguyen

2328
FROM MIDAS TOUCH
"We are what we believe. We believe what we think."
Dr. Bak Nguyen

2329
FROM MIDAS TOUCH
"Champions and heroes are average
within our ranks!"
Dr. Bak Nguyen

2330
FROM MIDAS TOUCH
"The discovery of science is bathed with doubt, but
not its application. Remember, we are white coats."
Dr. Bak Nguyen

2331
FROM MIDAS TOUCH
"As caregivers, we have the obligation
to believe first."
Dr. Bak Nguyen

2332
FROM MIDAS TOUCH
"We have worked too hard to fail happiness,
blinded by our desire to be right."
Dr. Bak Nguyen

2333
FROM MIDAS TOUCH
"He gave me a taste of their love
and I became a believer!"
Dr. Bak Nguyen

2334
FROM MIDAS TOUCH
"Don't go through it alone, you won't last."
Dr. Bak Nguyen

2335

"The surgical skills and the technics are only half of the equation. The other half starts with happiness."

Dr. Bak Nguyen

2336

"To most, the future is the only key,
the past holds no hope."

Dr. Bak Nguyen

2337

"We have already given!
Now we need to learn to receive."

Dr. Bak Nguyen

2338

"We have too much to achieve to be busy and ignore our own replenishment and rejuvenation."

Dr. Bak Nguyen

2339
FROM THE POWER OF DR
"As doctors, our title and training are the best tools to leverage ourselves out of this worldwide mess!"
Dr. Bak Nguyen

2340
FROM THE POWER OF DR
"Call me Doctor."
Dr. Bak Nguyen

2341
FROM THE POWER OF DR
"Very soon, weights become burdens."
Dr. Bak Nguyen

2342
FROM THE POWER OF DR
"You call me doctor to remind me to always put your interests before mine."
Dr. Bak Nguyen

2343
FROM THE POWER OF DR
"I found my speed, trying to escape pressure."
Dr. Bak Nguyen

2344
FROM THE POWER OF DR
"Trust is based on feelings."
Dr. Bak Nguyen

2345
FROM THE POWER OF DR
"Doubt will kill as hope will save."
Dr. Bak Nguyen

2346
FROM THE POWER OF DR
"Facing defeat, failure, even success, the image
looking back at you in the mirror is often
the richest source of raw data."
Dr. Bak Nguyen

2347
FROM THE POWER OF DR
"To keep believing, to keep delivering,
to keep pushing forward, no matter what.
That's overachieving."
Dr. Bak Nguyen

2348

"The power hack was from within our title."

Dr. Bak Nguyen

2349

"When the cliff is reached, the trust is breached…
and we are in trial."

Dr. Bak Nguyen

2350

"Until the cliff is reached, the cliff was a myth,
one we all heard of."

Dr. Bak Nguyen

2351

" As we were trained to be self-sustained and
independent, we are also confronted to the habits of
performance and perfection."

Dr. Bak Nguyen

2352
FROM THE POWER OF DR
"A doctor may be a title, a healer is the function."
Dr. Bak Nguyen

2353
FROM THE POWER OF DR
"Once happy, you are much more powerful,
as a healer!"
Dr. Bak Nguyen

2354
FROM THE CONFESSION OF AN OVERACHIEVER
"Taking care of someone else, you do not have to
deal with your own emotions, eliminating most of the
resistance to your growth."
Dr. Bak Nguyen

2355
FROM THE CONFESSION OF AN OVERACHIEVER
"The only way to help someone else
is to be secure first."
Dr. Bak Nguyen

2356

FROM THE CONFESSION OF AN OVERACHIEVER

"To be selfless, you must first be self-aware."

Dr. Bak Nguyen

This is **Shortcut volume 8, Doctor**. Welcome to the Alphas.

Dr. BAK NGUYEN

PART 3
"EVOLUTION"
by Dr. BAK NGUYEN

And what about **evolution**? Evolution at a broader scale is how we grow wiser as a species. Well, since our own growth has been severely handicapped by our profession, we need to double down on growth. That's what I felt and what I bet on. It is also how I have come to rise to now, be discussing with you.

What I call **evolution** is the growth that will serve the many. I needed to heal and I found ways to do so. To serve the many, I share back my findings in my writing and conferences. As a result, I grew even more and at a much higher pace and scope.

I rose with the ***leadership of empowerment***, looking to raise the average with me. I empower and listen to the person who received my attention. At that point, I am open, that person still needs to win my trust. That is the main difference with me judging, prior to my 18 months **YESMAN challenge**. I empower and I listen.

The great thing about empowerment, it amplifies everything. There is nowhere to hide. As much as your intentions and ambitions are gaining in power, so are your flaws and liabilities.

No one is perfect, that I know. But since I have that power to make things happen, I still have to see to whom I am lending such power.

And this is how I share and empower first, without judgment and then, I still need to read the data and to readjust. Some have taken my kindness and politeness as weaknesses to abuse, even using my own words against me as I am a man of my words.

Well, I empowered them and was genuine and truly hope that what was coming out was worth my time and yours. I opened up and empowered without judging first but then, as I see the truth, I asserted it and sorted out the good from the bad.

And what is good is what will help the many. What is bad is what will take too much time, vague and even exclusive. I am serving the average and the world, remember?

Any action that might raise the average is deemed good to me. Then, I still need to assert the odds and the time required. You won't see me spending my entire life on one issue.

I choose my battles and still have to keep my momentum going from win to win. That's the blessing I received from God, that is also what I have to deliver on.

So about my word? I have never say this to anyone in their face, always trying to keep some hope alive but the truth is that: "I will keep my word and more if you are worth it.

Otherwise, you have a great opening with me and you blew it. The loss is yours! I am still very grateful to have seen your real face that soon in the process. I wish you luck."

I am not saying that this is the process of evolution, it is mine. Personal growth brought me that far, to keep rising, I need to empower more and more people. This was also how I got inspired from my training as a doctor: I empower to heal. Their healing was my gift. Because I gave, I grew. What a great formula, don't you think?

And this is the formula that will be of great use to you, all of you, white coats! Give and be open to grow. Personal growth and skill improvement have taken you that far. To rise above the glass ceiling (the level between belonging and esteem in the Pyramid of Maslow), you need to serve and to be open to grow. That's your evolution.

SELF-ACTUALIZATION

ESTEEM

LOVE/BELONGING

SAFETY

`PHYSIOLOGICAL NEEDS`

THE PYRAMID OF ABRAHAM MASLOW

If, to the world, it was personal growth since the world will heal at the pace of our growth, this is part of evolution. Think with me. What happens when you are healing someone, giving them back the gift of life and the hope of a future? The good deeds of that person will also appear on your ledger.

And what happens when you healed a monster? Well, it was not our place to judge. We heal without prejudice, hoping that the goodness of our heart will heal that person both physically and morally. We do our best, their choices are not ours to bear!

And this is the beauty of our profession, our passion. Everyone has a chance to heal and to rethink their choices and goals. We brought them to the **readjustment phase**. After that point, well, that's above our pay grade.

And you know what? I am blessed that it is not within my pay grade to wonder. It took me 40 years to understand, but each time that I am judging, I chipped away a little piece of my soul. So you can guess how fast I have put an end to this kind of practice.

I do not judge. I help, I empower and then, I readjust. I am a doctor, and so are you. I am not just talking figuratively here. This is also how I treat my patients. I am a dental cosmetic surgeon, the teeth, the smile and the harmony of the face are my fields of expertise, right? According to my dental license, it is correct.

In truth, people come to me to gain confidence. They just happened to focus on one physical aspect to express their lack of confidence. Well, I listen and will tell them how I can *fix* the issue. It is very important that they are part of the process.

Even if to me, I saw the solution within the first 10 seconds of our encounter, I still need to give them the time to figure out what is their problem and what can be done to solve it.

Then, I empower them with all of myself, lending them my skills, experience, and knowledge. Together, we have to picture clearly the outcome, within the first consultation. And if we both agree, then I started the prerequisites.

As the treatment is advancing, I always involve my patients to keep them informed on the advancement of the process, which is their journey. I always keep that in mind, to they it was a journey, with a story, dreams and maybe, drama.

They are in control, with me as a partner and coach. More than once, I had the privilege of seeing people blooming with confidence through their journey with me.

My hands and skill fixed their smile, my kindness and warmth help their confidence. Today, people are still coming to me to fix their teeth, that's my license as a doctor. I never promise anything more. In truth, I found a way to empower each of them to heal their healing process.

Those are will be growing and rising, I will have shared a part of their story. Some will require more before reaching such a state. To them, I still have given my best. And this is what I am doing as a doctor, with the DR in front of my name.

And what about **evolution**? Well, helping more and more people, I could not help but to see patterns emerging. These patterns showed me a world of logic and of possibilities to read the world and the future.

Rest assured, I am no James Bond's villain. First, I never share in any book the content of my discussion with any of my patients. Secondly, I have shared back to all of you what I have discovered walking that path.

The best synthesis of my work is the journey of **SHORTCUT**, all 8 the volumes. To bet on myself to better myself, to serve to grow, and to raise the average by sharing, that, to me, is evolution. This, to me, is **leadership**!

"The day one is raising the average instead of beating it, that day, one has joined leadership."
Dr. Bak Nguyen

And that is the power within each of you my brothers and sisters, doctors and white coats. You already bear the weight of the world on your shoulder. Is that okay if I help you to ease your pain? For you, sure, but especially for the sake of all of those, you will be helping.

For a white coat, your personal growth is evolution at the scale of society. Remember that and take care of yourself. Be kind and generous, to others and to you too. That is also part of your engagement, to do no harm!

The world still needs you! Now more than ever.

This is **Shortcut volume 8, Doctor**. Welcome to the Alphas.

Remember, you treat the present and the future, not the past.

Dr. BAK NGUYEN

PART 4

"81 EVOLUTION QUOTES"

by Dr. BAK NGUYEN

1284

FROM LEADERSHIP, PANDORA'S BOX

"The secret of the evolution of mankind lays
in the wisdom of working together."

Dr. Bak Nguyen

1285

FROM IDENTITY, ANTHOLOGY OF QUESTS

"We were animals who learned to sing.
And then, we became humans."

Dr. Bak Nguyen

1286

FROM IDENTITY, ANTHOLOGY OF QUESTS

"In the past we tried to standardize everything.
Today we should stop and decide who we are.
So we can customize our future..."

Dr. Bak Nguyen

1287

FROM PROFESSION HEALTH

"After our whole, our kind!
Let us stop being apes!"

Dr. Bak Nguyen

1288
FROM AMONGST THE ALPHAS, VOLUME 2
"Fears transmitted are mostly the boundaries
of the last generation."
Dr. Bak Nguyen

1289
FROM INDUSTRIES' DISRUPTORS
"It seems that human evolution is finally catching up
with the evolution of the cpu."
Dr. Bak Nguyen

1290
FROM INDUSTRIES' DISRUPTORS
"The Internet has empowered
the era of entrepreneurs!"
Dr. Bak Nguyen

1291
FROM INDUSTRIES' DISRUPTORS
"If it can be improved, what are we waiting for?
Everyone will benefit from it!"
Dr. Bak Nguyen

1292

FROM INDUSTRIES' DISRUPTORS

"Today, keynote speakers are filling
the gap left between our universities and
the evolution of life and technology."
Dr. Bak Nguyen

1293

FROM AMONGST THE ALPHAS, VOLUME 2

"Millennials are evolution and natural selection
proclaiming their progression
on the pyramid of Maslow!"
Dr. Bak Nguyen

1294

FROM AMONGST THE ALPHAS, VOLUME 2

"Were angels a different species created by God or
the relics of an old memory of our own kind?"
Dr. Bak Nguyen

1295

FROM INDUSTRIES' DISRUPTORS

"The new is still unproven, but today, it is sexy!"
Dr. Bak Nguyen

1296
FROM INDUSTRIES' DISRUPTORS
"What were once hidden parts of the story are today
the frontline of your story."
Dr. Bak Nguyen

1297
FROM CHANGING THE WORLD FROM A DENTAL CHAIR
" People change, you change,
respect that and deal with it."
Dr. Bak Nguyen

1298
FROM THE POWER BEHIND THE ALPHA
" A heart does not evolve,
it simply grows and retracts."
Dr. Bak Nguyen

1299
FROM THE POWER BEHIND THE ALPHA
"It was easier to discover novelty
than to filter the old."
Dr. Bak Nguyen

1300

FROM REBOOT, TO GROW FROM MIDLIFE CRISIS

"Time and Space change everything.
To stay relevant, we must evolve."

Dr. Bak Nguyen

1301

FROM REBOOT, TO GROW FROM MIDLIFE CRISIS

"Averaging down... that's not evolution,
it's extinction, from an evolution's standpoint."

Dr. Bak Nguyen

1302

FROM LEVERAGE COMMUNICATION INTO SUCCESS

"No one really changes, we simply evolve
and gain more nuances."

Dr. Bak Nguyen

1303

FROM LEVERAGE COMMUNICATION INTO SUCCESS

"Our body will adapt by reducing the production of
the hormonal respond as technology will compensate
by increases its pace and reach."

Dr. Bak Nguyen

1304

FROM LEVERAGE COMMUNICATION INTO SUCCESS

"The new is neither good or bad.
It can be great if you take the time to master it."

Dr. Bak Nguyen

1305

FROM FORCES OF NATURE

"To keep evolving, comfort zones are oasis to replenish at, then, the journey continues."

Dr. Bak Nguyen

1306

FROM THE BOOK OF LEGENDS, VOLUME 1

"As immigrants kids, proving yourself
is always somewhere on the table,
hardwired into our core beliefs..."

Dr. Bak Nguyen

1307

FROM SELFMADE

"You can't stand IN the way of evolution.
You can help or stand aside, the choice is yours."

Dr. Bak Nguyen

1308
FROM SELFMADE

"The main trade that we should transmit is
the mean to adapt, the desire to reshape and
the ability to ask questions. "

Dr. Bak Nguyen

1309
FROM KRYPTO

" To eat was good enough to the animal kingdom.
To be happy is the legacy of human evolution."

Dr. Bak Nguyen

1310
FROM KRYPTO

" Evolution and Legacy are what
should united all of us "

Dr. Bak Nguyen

1311
FROM KRYPTO

" Evolution rather than revolution.
It will required, wisdom and flexibility,
not just determination and courage."

Dr. Bak Nguyen

1312
FROM KRYPTO
" Feel to learn. This time, it wasn't that expensive."
Dr. Bak Nguyen

1313
FROM KRYPTO
"So let's be better than animals and take the survival
part out of the equation once and for all."
Dr. Bak Nguyen

1314
FROM KRYPTO
"The human factor of life is to thrive,
the animal side is to survive."
Dr. Bak Nguyen

1315
FROM POWER, EMOTIONAL INTELLIGENCE
"Like anything else,
gathered intelligence has an expiration date."
Dr. Bak Nguyen

1316

FROM POWER, EMOTIONAL INTELLIGENCE

"Even if the ocean is much closer to us, it was easier to reach out in space than to dive deep in the ocean."

Dr. Bak Nguyen

1317

FROM THE POWER OF YES, VOLUME 1

"We attract what we genuinely are."

Dr. Bak Nguyen

1318

FROM HORIZON VOLUME TWO

"The evolution is within the unknown and the new. If your future is proven, you are mainly rewriting the past, once more."

Dr. Bak Nguyen

1319

FROM HORIZON VOLUME TWO

"The only way to evolve is to adapt."

Dr. Bak Nguyen

1320

"Human evolution has come to an age
that the one holding the sword is now the target,
not the king anymore."

Dr. Bak Nguyen

1321
FROM HUMILITY FOR SUCCESS
"To be humble is to be aware of our changing place
in a bigger and forever changing Universe."

Dr. Bak Nguyen

1322
FROM HUMILITY FOR SUCCESS
"If you want to bet on a sure value, bet on change!"

Dr. Bak Nguyen

1323
FROM THE ENERGY FORMULA
"Our fore and founding fathers were very clever
to build values into our Identity."

Dr. Bak Nguyen

1324
FROM THE ENERGY FORMULA
"The layers of civilization started to weight on our primary goal and instincts. It never stopped doubling down its control since."

Dr. Bak Nguyen

1325
FROM THE ENERGY FORMULA
"No one had to teach us how to eat, to seek shelter or to have sex. Those were hardwired."

Dr. Bak Nguyen

1326
FROM SUCCESS IS A CHOICE
"To evolve is much easier than to change. but often, that wasn't a choice. it was just the timing."

Dr. Bak Nguyen

1327
FROM THE 90 DAYS CHALLENGE
"The flaw in the system is the by default."

Dr. Bak Nguyen

1328
FROM THE 90 DAYS CHALLENGE
"Acting by default will kill us all while we are asleep at the wheel."

Dr. Bak Nguyen

1329
FROM RISING
"Evolution does not always
come with great feelings. "
Dr. Bak Nguyen

1330
FROM RISING
"No one can stand in front of evolution,
just like no one can resist the power of time.
So, the only smart alternative left is to provoke
and ride evolution and time."
Dr. Bak Nguyen

1331
FROM AFTERMATH
"Changing is never something we welcome easily."
Dr. Bak Nguyen

1332
FROM AFTERMATH
"The paradox of our evolution is to have grown
into a collective of individuals."
Dr. Bak Nguyen

1333

FROM AFTERMATH

"Better a smaller change that will last
than a in-dept one that will fade."

Dr. Bak Nguyen

1334

FROM AFTERMATH

"Adapting their mastery to the present
and immediate needs is reinventing."

Dr. Bak Nguyen

1335

FROM RELEVANCY

"For the first time within our lifetime, all interests
aligned. The age of competition is over,
the age of collaboration has begun."

Dr. Bak Nguyen

1336

FROM MIDAS TOUCH

"Habit does not go with evolution.
Comfort does not go with evolution."

Dr. Bak Nguyen

1337
FROM TORNADO
"The world is changing, with or without you.
At best, you are adapting forward."
Dr. Bak Nguyen

1338
FROM TORNADO
"Never underestimate the idle instinct of people."
Dr. Bak Nguyen

1339
FROM TORNADO
"Real lasting change is a flow, not an impact."
Dr. Bak Nguyen

1340
FROM TORNADO
"An idea is an impact. A philosophy is a flow.
One will last, one will be swallowed."
Dr. Bak Nguyen

1341
FROM TORNADO
"Change must be inspired,
not imposed to be sustainable."
Dr. Bak Nguyen

1342

FROM BOOTCAMP

"Evolution is not about accumulating
but about experiencing."

Dr. Bak Nguyen

1343

FROM THE UAX STORY

"I understood that a change, to be sustainable
has to be kind and sensitive to its own impact,
good and collateral."

Dr. Bak Nguyen

1344

FROM 1SELF

"It is always time to change, but somehow,
it is never the right timing."

Dr. Bak Nguyen

1345

FROM 1SELF

"Moving up, the air might be scarcer,
but in exchange, you gain horizon and perspective,
leading you to clarity."

Dr. Bak Nguyen

1346

FROM 1SELF

"If you are more than you have, changing direction
to adapt to the flow of life should not be
that big of a challenge."

Dr. Bak Nguyen

1347

FROM ALPHA LADDERS VOLUME 2

"We all do, we change, we evolve.
How long will that ORDER stay relevant?"

Dr. Bak Nguyen

1348

FROM ALPHA LADDERS VOLUME 2

"Ambition is the motor of evolution, after surviving."

Dr. Bak Nguyen

1349

FROM ALPHA LADDERS VOLUME 2

"So ambition is good! It is what's driving the world."

Dr. Bak Nguyen

1350
FROM ALPHA LADDERS VOLUME 2
"The purpose of Life was to evolve and to adapt,
not to freeze the world within a picture
and to bonzai its growth."
Dr. Bak Nguyen

1351
FROM ALPHA LADDERS VOLUME 2
"Ambition is not bad. On the contrary,
it is a very powerful leverage when empowered."
Dr. Bak Nguyen

1352
FROM ALPHA LADDERS VOLUME 2
"The compassion to evolve with no resistance
and fewer collaterals, we are ready for that."
Dr. Bak Nguyen

1353
FROM ALPHA LADDERS VOLUME 2
"To Evolve is to Change. Change causes Resistance."
Dr. Bak Nguyen

1354

"Evolution is smooth without pride.
The second part is obvious and yet
so hard to achieve."

Dr. Bak Nguyen

1355

FROM MIRRORS

"Evolution is a lonely path."

Dr. Bak Nguyen

1356

FROM MIRRORS

"To be ready to be mentored is to accept
to surrender our own insecurities."

Dr. Bak Nguyen

1357

FROM MIRRORS

"Evolution is a pain, the pain to change."

Dr. Bak Nguyen

1358

"The course of evolution eventually
will divert from the path of happiness."

Dr. Bak Nguyen

1359

FROM MIRRORS

"When a student rebels from his teacher,
it is often because the pain was higher
than the foreseeable benefits."

Dr. Bak Nguyen

1360

FROM MIRRORS

"Even nature, in other words, God,
has to try and fail to find balance."

Dr. Bak Nguyen

1361

FROM TO OVERACHIEVE EVERYTHING BEING LAZY

"With both our feet firmly planted in the past,
the future is not that easily accessible.
Even less changeable."

Dr. Bak Nguyen

1362

"If an opportunity and a risk were both different faces of the same coin, challenge is the coin."

Dr. Bak Nguyen

1363

"The later one faces a challenge, the great is the ratio risk/opportunity."

Dr. Bak Nguyen

1364

"We evolve, we do not change."

Dr. Bak Nguyen

This is **Shortcut volume 8, Doctor**. Welcome to the Alphas.

Remember, you beat the present and the future, not the past.

Dr. BAK NGUYEN

PART 5
"THE POWER OF QUOTES"
by Dr. BAK NGUYEN

This is my last **POWER OF QUOTE** chapter of this franchise. I must say that after 7 of these supercharged chapters with an average of twice to three times the average length of my usual chapters, I came to fear the **POWER OF QUOTE** time.

Yes, I am lazy and I am not shy to admit it. That said, I will keep pushing. Why? Because if for me it is a few extra hours writing, to you, it is a shortcut of years of experiences and mistakes.

Yes, I had more than my fair share of mistakes. Nobody is perfect and I will be the first one to admit that. That said, I made mistakes, I failed, and most importantly, I learnt. And this is what it is all about, learning and growing.

Since the day I stopped looking to be right but to win instead, I rose, almost with ease. The imagery is very concise here, this is about cutting your anchors and to start rising.

And what is an anchor? Well, most of the anchors I cut were false beliefs and pride. I would love to say that I got rid of everything, but I am really trying my best. What is for sure is that I am much less burden today than before my awakening. Today, I am whole and lighter. How about that?

And what helped me to achieve such transformations? A continuous change in mindsets and views. No, I am not changing my mind with the winds, I reevaluate the winds and adapt.

What is true today within our scope may not be as true tomorrow or even yesterday. We need to ask the question and find the answer, time and time again until we got tired of that specific question.

What I found doing so is that whatever questions I am still raising, even after the answers, those are my next journey and adventures to grow from. Those questions that I know the answer by heart, well, I stopped bother and leave them at home.

"Make leverage of your liabilities"
Dr. Bak Nguyen

I told you that to move as fast as far and for as long, one has to keep light. Well, my knowledge, wins and medals, those are part of the past. Unless I can leverage the past to build my next bridge, that is excess weight. The only past that I am carrying around is Gratitude.

"Gratitude is the only past with a future."
Dr. Bak Nguyen

This also explains how I came up with more than 2500 quotes within the last 4 years. I am still looking for the answer, of how to heal, of how to be better, of how to be more, of how to be happier… What I found, I shared with you.

A quote at a time, I changed my life. A quote at a time, I improved my conditions and I found my powers. A quote at a time, I gave and received. This is what **the power of quote** has done for me, to be able to do more within the last 4 years than in my first 40.

Trust me on this. Each day, read 4 quotes and let them sink in. The next day, do the same. Within 3 months, you will see how far you will have walked these journeys you keep pushing down the road. Ever heard of the saying: "Life is what happens why we are busy planning…"?

Well, we are not just busy planning… we are just busy turning in circle because we were told to do so. Well, the awakening will change all of that. The healing will bring closure and you will be ready to grow.

About cutting down the anchors and to move lightweight, I know that you will need more to be convinced. I invite all of you to look for **THE ENERGY FORMULA**, my 53rd book, both the doctor and the scientist in you will be satisfied with the answers and explanations.

In the meantime, let's travel once more the journey of 8 of these famous quotes. I made a special selection for this volume, you will be retracing my steps as a doctor looking for his voice and identity while trying his best not to revolt and spit on everything that came before and everything he worked so hard for.

FAMOUS QUOTE 1

0015
FROM CHANGING THE WORLD FROM A DENTAL CHAIR
"Mdex, for joy for life."
Dr. Bak Nguyen

That is the slogan of my company, Mdex. Well, to be perfectly honest, this one arrived on the table 8 years after the existence of Mdex. The first one was **Mdex, rethinking health.**

I was fresh out of school and was still looking to compensate for the opportunity I walked away from, Hollywood. I had much to prove and even more to lose not to succeed. That was very cerebral, almost pretentious.

It took me a year to finally accept my choices and condition, and to become a good doctor to my patients. Very quickly, the difference that I was achieving on the field was surely not one that I could have thought of.

I was miserable as a dentist. Add on top of that that Hollywood's doors were within reach… the regrets made me into a ghost. On the verge of bankruptcy, after betting everything I had opening up my own clinic, I got a dose of humility, a dose of reality. I realized that it was now too late to look back.

Looking back for a whole year put my present and future in danger. So I made peace with my decision and signed a contract with myself for 10 years.

For 10 years, I will be the best dentist I can be, only after 10 years, I will have the option to revisit what I left behind.

That solves the regret and haunting problem. I was still miserable in my dental chair. Then, patients started to show up. Talking with them distracted me from my own sorrow. Helping them to solve their pain, I felt better too. I was then that I realize how easier it is to solve others' problem since my emotions are not involved.

I solved their teeth and health problems but that was not enough to keep me from being miserable. Every time that I had a patient in my chair, they did not like to be there and me neither. We connected on that. And I found friendships that I could never see coming.

But for the first year that was disastrous, I became a successful dentist, one people loved and were sending referrals to. Soon, the clinic became too small for the practice that I have built. We planned for an expansion.

I was 7 years into my own contract, it was too soon to revisit my **option** but the planning of a new clinic allowed the opportunity to see the future and to assert where I was going. Even if the question was about the future, I looked at the past 7 years and acknowledge to what I owe my success: my love for people.

After a night or two sleeping on the matter, **Mdex, for joy for life** became the new slogan of the company. I don't think that it requires more explanation. Just know that as quote, **Mdex, for joy for life,** brought my company to a company level, one looking at its chance for a national expansion and even an IPO, initial public offering.

If you were looking for the power of a quote, here is my life example.

FAMOUS QUOTE 2

0032

FROM SELFMADE

"Knowledge is the ground of the past.
Hope and dreams are the air of the future."

Dr. Bak Nguyen

Having fled my ghost status looking back on my regrets, I kept my mind where it felt secure, looking forward. That was the only direction I could look at, without asking too many answerless questions or reopening old wounds.

Everything that I needed to do, what I need to learn, all the answers were ahead. Even as a dentist, what I learnt back from school, I renewal more than half of it. Most of the operations I am now carrying, I learnt the art and craft after graduation. So why bother so much with the past? Especially that the past is where my ghost and demons lay.

Basically, I was fleeing instead of facing. That worked pretty well. I know what you will say, that eventually, I will have to stop and face my own demons. Well, you know what? I did that, years later, but I grew so much and as I stopped feeding my demons, they shrunk so much that they were now the size of tiny insects.

"My demons, I did not have to deal with them,
I just need to stop feeding them my life force."
Dr. Bak Nguyen

That's quote #2525. The day I understood that concept of feeding and starving, everything in Life became clear. This is what the bible was trying to teach us talking about statue of salt if we turned back to look behind.

In Greek mythology, the is a similar legend as Orpheus went to the underworld to save his wife, Eurydice, and as they were about to reach the surface, turned back and looked at her, then, she vanished…

Even the concept of haunting and ghosts is teaching us to move on if we do not to be trapped in the past. Around that time, the internet exploded and Google became the new encyclopedia, the newspapers were in trouble and YouTube was the new name in town.

Things are changing and changing fast. Do you want to ride the change or to be caught under the waves?

7 years ago, I made my peace with my regrets. This time, it was easy, to move forward was simple and without any new wounds or separations.

I moved forward, as a dentist, as a CEO, and as a man. I keep with me what I need to cross the next bridge and stay grateful for what I received. If anything, I now need to deliver, to give back, to honour. All of those happen in the future.

14 years later, I must say that the same mindset keeps pushing me forward with momentum, style, and ease.

FAMOUS QUOTE 3

0041

FROM POWER, EMOTIONAL INTELLIGENCE

"I believe in myself, and I do it for God,
not the other way around."

Dr. Bak Nguyen

This one is one of my favourite. The wording is pretty clear but here is the story behind that one. I spent all of the Sundays of my childhood at the church with my parents. I knew the bible inside and out.

Then, I grew up and somehow outgrew the belief of my parents. In God, I trust but I stopped listening to the church and its priests.

Almost 20 years later, I will have the chance to visit ROME and the St-Peter Basilica. I did not find any sign of God there, that I can tell you. Instead, I can still smell the blood and almost hear the scream of the atrocities carried in his name. So no, I have no regret.

That said, my religious education taught me fear, much fear. Well, I leveraged that legacy and made it into something special, useful.

In the bible, the is a story about a master and his three servants. The master left for a year. Before leaving, he called his servants and gave 3 talents to the first one, 2 to the second one, and 1 to the last servant.

A year later, the master came back and asked for his due. The first servant ran to him and greeted him with 6 talents, the 3 he received and 3 in profits. In Roman times, money was talent… (or was it a word play to trick with our minds?) Anyway, the second servant presented his 2 + 2 talents.

Looking at his colleagues, the last one went out on the field to dig up the talent that we received. He was so scared of losing that unique talent that he buried it. Now, he was giving it back, all rusty and soiled. The master kicked out the lazy and bad servant and gave that talent to the one with 6 already.

Well, that night, I dreamed of being in front of Saint-Peter and walking with him the corridors leading to my final trial. I was confident. Then, I present myself in front of God and present the 3 talents that I received and the 3 more I created.

God, too surprised to be angry, stood up and looking down on me saying: "What are you talking about? I gave you 10!"

I woke up completely in sweat. I was out of time. I never forgot that warning. Since that night, I run and run fast to no run out of time in front of God. This particular fear has somehow overwritten all of my other fears.

And this is the leverage I got from my religious education and from that nightmare. I managed to push the only fear I have into the next life… How about that for a mindset, for leverage? Now you have the quote.

So now, I run and deliver on my talents. I do that serving others. Every time that I succeed, I found even more talents. The writing was one of the new talents I found walking my journey. I am amazed and happy for a moment until I realized that I will have to deliver on that one too!

No time to waste, I keep betting on myself (the talents that I have received) but I run to honour God, that's the fear that keeps me pushing for more, always more.

0046

FROM THE POWER OF YES, VOLUME 1

"Speed is my power. Momentum, my expression."

Dr. Bak Nguyen

By now, you should know that I am addicted to my own speed. Throughout the journey of the 8 volumes of **SHORTCUT**, I shared with you the secret of my speed. With the last anecdote, you now know the WHY too.

I run to not run out of time. I run and jump from win to win. With the **GAMER MENTALITY**, I cross my checkpoints and pace up from there. In my medical career, I treat a patient at a time. From one success to the next, I built a career and a prosperous company, one people look for.

And if you don't stop, well, your wins are adding up faster than you can count, pushing your rise not by adding up but by an exponential factor. If you want a clear example, just look at my books and their numbers. Looking forward, I can still understand and plan. Looking back, I got vertigo every single time.

There are still books that I haven't published yet within those written within the first 2 years. They are written, I just need to go back to them and publish them. That has proven to be a pain in the a**.

Since last year, I have invented the **COMBO** format with the **ECHO protocol**, allowing the production of a printed book and an audiobook in parallel and having Amazon and Barnes & Noble to distribute them. I have successfully made most of the books I wrote from that point on, with the **COMBO formula**.

It might take me years before I could upgrade my entire library. Why? Because looking forward is cleaner and easier for me. Sorting out of the past, what a mess! Especially with so many titles to compile!

So I am fast, I am speed. That's my power. With my mindset of jumping from win to win, always leveraging on the last one to keep propelling myself, momentum became the ripple effect of my journey. Today, my momentum is such that it is easier for me to keep going than to stop.

Jumping from win to win, afraid of running out of time. That's how I express myself before having to face God.

FAMOUS QUOTE 5

0048
FROM HOW TO NOT FAIL AS A DENTIST
"Changing the world from a dental chair."

Dr. Bak Nguyen

This became the first signature phrase of Dr. Bak. I never really thought of that one. It came to me as I was giving a speech to a crowd of business students and entrepreneurs at the John Molson School of Business, Concordia University.

We were talking about what it takes to stand up for your dreams and to change the world. Then, I took the microphone and said: "If I have changed the world from a dental chair, you are all in a better position than I am to change the world!"

I said that to empower the crowd to follow their dreams and vision just like I followed mine, despite all the odds stacked against me. Well, that phrase became my signature as Dr. Bak. Years later, as I travelled the street of Montreal, people still stopped me, recognizing me from that speech.

CHANGING THE WORLD FROM A DENTAL CHAIR also became the title of the book I wrote to defend my nomination as Ernst and Young, Entrepreneur of the year. That brought me more than attention, it brought me the favour of the financial world, more than once!

That was before my rise as a world record author and, later on, a world anchor. Just like **RETHINKING HEALTH**, it was a first signature to tell the world of my existence. Just like that one was eventually replaced with **Mdex, for joy for life**, **CHANGING THE WORLD FROM A DENTAL CHAIR** will be replaced with **WELCOME TO THE ALPHAS**.

In both cases, I started with the affirmation of myself and evolved to replace it with a promise, including you. **Mdex, for joy for life**, is a promise, one people believe in. **Welcome to the Alphas**, can you think of an even better inclusive promise?

It has to start with you and then, branch out. That's the only way to be genuine If you follow my teaching throughout the **SHORTCUT series**, I told you to be Confident and to believe in yourself first. You serve and then, you readjust. That is exactly my process, not once but twice, with Mdex and then, with Dr. Bak.

Changing the world, that I will keep doing until I die, that's my debt to God. From a dental chair, well, I guess that after 20 years in the profession, I will never be too far from a dental chair, even if life is leading me to new horizons. I will always keep the DR as gratitude and as a reminder, that's for sure.

FAMOUS QUOTE 6

0056
FROM PLAYBOOK INTRODUCTION VOLUME 2
"Reach for your next win as soon as possible, and build on it!"
Dr. Bak Nguyen

This is the essence of my momentum and most predominant power. Jumping from win to win, I utilized the energy and resources of one win as a launching pad for the next one. So no, I will not stay long for the celebrations.

I will be celebrating my wins as I exchange with my new teammates, strapped in the rocket to the next mission. We will laugh, we will smile, and then, soon enough, the new mission will require all of our attention.

Talking about the last win is the best way to motivate your new team and to keep their attention when doubt and procrastination could kill the new launch. And yes, I change team between the mission, it is almost impossible for one to keep going at my pace. That said, some faces are back, mission after mission, with some break in between.

On some missions, I fly solo. That's cool. And even in solo, I still talk about my last win, just to keep doubts and fatigue at bay. That is how, moving from win to win, I built my momentum.

I wrote book after book, a chapter at a time. From that momentum, I reached the world of audiobooks and printing. I got accepted by the big three who are publishing my books within hours of their submissions. I have also convinced Amazon and Barnes and Noble to carry my format of **COMBO PAPERBACK/AUDIOBOOK**, which is a world first.

I did not stop there. I went back on my steps, in my past life as a movie producer to get the needed inspiration to produce a new kind of audiobooks, blockbuster audiobooks which are basically a movie without images to keep the audience engaged, visual and auditive people alike. Those are called **U.A.X, Ultimate Audio Experience**. They are now distributed by all the major outlets and streaming on Apple Music, Spotify, and Amazon. How about that from jumping from win to win?

And dentistry? Well, I am today at the top of my game, treating patients. Lately, my new challenge is to pass on that knowledge and trust to other dentists. That, I am still working on.

About our projects and expansion, if with the shadow that COVID has cast on everything, we are opening a new complex next month. And a bank is already looking to finance our next expansion… A win at a time.

I went from a beloved dentist to a successful dentist. From one dentist with the favour of the financial world to a **world TOP100 doctor**. I don't know what the future holds but I know I am pacing up and going faster and faster.

And these are the wins. What about the losses? Well, those I carry around until I have a chance for a rematch.

"I will learn until I win. As I win, I move on."
Dr. Bak Nguyen

That's quote #2526. That's about the wins. Now about the speed? Do you remember how we survived all the long exams back in Dental and Med school, especially when there were 100 of them?

Well, you jump to the next question if you don't have the answer. You have 50% of the chance that the answer you seek will be within the next questions. Well, I used the same strategy in my life, and guess what, the odds are way better than 50%!

Those questions I skipped are the failure that I carry around and will come back to eventually. Some people call that closure, others will call it stubbornness. To me, it is about winning and timing. I will learn until I win.

"To always move forward,
make leverage of your liabilities."
Dr. Bak Nguyen

FAMOUS QUOTE 7

0050
FROM HOW TO NOT FAIL AS A DENTIST
"With your money, do not trust anyone but yourself."
Dr. Bak Nguyen

This one is very specific. I am addressing everyone but this is particularly true with doctors. We are smart and we are making a good income. That said, why are we often referred to as the dump money of most markets?

Sit down with a banker and have a glass or two of great wine. Shut up and listen. You will realize that as a client, you are the best. But none of them will want you as a partner. Why is that?

Because we are glorified workers whose titles went to our head. I know about leadership and about delegating. But you can only delegate what you have first mastered. Does that make sense to you?

The problem with us is that we know that we are smart but we swallow the crap that we can't be good in everything and then, we trust the experts. Well, the experts are good once you tell them what to do, not to tell you what to do with your money!

So I will urge all of you to take the time to understand the rules, the numbers, and the game before delegating. Sure, there are better people to handle money. But that's your money! Will you leave your kids to experts you just met? … Oh wait, that is also what we do too!

The first rule of delegation is trust and verify. Are you? With our discipline and mindset, there is nothing that we can't understand, we just need to see its importance.

You worked hard for your money. Make sure that it works hard for you. And for that, there is no cheat, you will need to educate yourself. But wait, to educate ourselves, isn't that one of our greatest strengths?

0060
FROM SUCCESS IS A CHOICE
"To succeed, be flexible."
Dr. Bak Nguyen

This will seem obvious. Don't be fooled by the appearances. To have done it, I can tell you that this might be one of the hardest things you will try. We all have pride, training, and habits. Changing will not come easily.

Well, our training made us elite and skilled surgeons. There are layers of rules upon layers of rules. To be flexible was never part of any of these layers, and yet, it might be the most important skill to master to survive and thrive.

To break my mind and habit, I had to enter 18 months of therapy, saying **YES** to almost everything. That reset my mind and I got freed from judging others, events, and even from judging myself.

If as a medical doctor, it is not easy to see how flexibility plays in our everyday tasks, well, being in business is always about dancing with the changes and waves. If you think that this is hard, well COVID will bring the game to a whole other level.

During the last months of COVID, we all experienced how things can shift quickly within an instant. People victims of war will all tell you the same. Those who will survive are those who will adapt, the fastest and the better. Well, in change, there is no better, until the change settles. So all there is left is how fast can you adapt?

You adapt and you readjust. Your first response will rarely be the good answer. The right answer is to stop waiting for things to come back as before.

The faster you can move out of denial, the better your chances of survival. In the worse case, you will be ridiculed by others pointing out your paranoia. You are still alive to tell the tale. Be grateful.

I am nothing close to someone who will easily panic. I had my painful experiences of reacting after the facts and dealing with the consequences too. Those are not fun at all. I learnt my lessons.

Today, I know that change is coming. From where and at what pace, those are the only unknown. I am not ready to wait for that change to come, I am not very good standing and waiting.

Some changes I see coming because I see the problem on the ground. Some other changes I feel. Well, if people lie, my instincts never lie to me. So today, I am often surfing the change even before the arrival of the **massive tsunami**.

I was the first one talking about space sharing and time-sharing for the dental space. That got me the attention and favour of the finance industry.

Well, after COVID, we all understood the liability that our boutique office represents and consequently, the high cost of dental care. We would be blind not to acknowledge that.

I was working these trails when COVID happened. It wasn't easy but I found my way through and emerge as a solution to now, an established problem, especially from the financial point of view.

In the book industry, I came in as an outsider. I had no attachment, just the need to get a book published. I got rejected. That did not stop me. On the contrary, I kept writing, not as a retaliation but that would be a great story to tell.

I kept writing, I learnt about publishing only to realize that people do not read as much anymore, especially the younger generations. Well, those are my primary audience!

So I adapted my medium to introduce the **COMBO PAPERBACK/AUDIOBOOK** format and the **U.A.X.** format. Once more, I am at the forefront of change.

And what is next? I don't know yet but I know that it will be fun, it will be huge and that I will do it! I can do it became today, I am flexible, I got rid of my insecurity, most of my identity and I can now yield flexibility with confidence and wisdom.

You don't have to start with flexibility. Start by opening up your mind and heart and grow from there. Soon enough, flexibility will come next on your list.

You wanted to break the curse and the routine? This is your chance! You wanted more and better? Be ready to embrace change, to drop your anchors and to rise. The wording is clear and straightforward. Read this paragraph again and you will know what is coming next!

This is **Shortcut volume 8, Doctor**. Welcome to the Alphas.

Dr. BAK NGUYEN

PART 10
"FAMOUS QUOTES"
by Dr. BAK NGUYEN

0001

FROM SYMPHONY OF SKILLS

"The pain of the problem has to be greater than the pain of change."

Dr. Bak Nguyen

0002

FROM SYMPHONY OF SKILLS

"Sharing is the way to grow."

Dr. Bak Nguyen

0003

FROM LEADERSHIP, PANDORA'S BOX

"One's legend can only begin the day one's Quest of Identity is over."

Dr. Bak Nguyen

0004

FROM IDENTITY, ANTHOLOGY OF QUESTS

"Gratitude is the only past with a future."

Dr. Bak Nguyen

0005

FROM PROFESSION HEALTH

"Mine was, forgive yourself."

Dr. Bak Nguyen

0006
FROM INDUSTRIES' DISRUPTORS
"To walk on thin ice is a dangerous game.
To run is safer. To surf is the easiest."
Dr. Bak Nguyen

0007
FROM INDUSTRIES' DISRUPTORS
"If I have changed the world from a dental chair,
you are all in a better position than I am
to change the world."
Dr. Bak Nguyen

0008
FROM INDUSTRIES' DISRUPTORS
"The day you are fighting to raise the average instead
of beating it, that day, you've joined the leadership."
Dr. Bak Nguyen

0009
FROM INDUSTRIES' DISRUPTORS
"At the end of the day, business is communication."
Dr. Bak Nguyen

0010
FROM INDUSTRIES' DISRUPTORS
"Make leverage of each of your liabilities,
and you will always be moving forward."
Dr. Bak Nguyen

0011
FROM INDUSTRIES' DISRUPTORS
"I believe in myself and I do it for God,
not the other way around."
Dr. Bak Nguyen

0012
FROM INDUSTRIES' DISRUPTORS
"Always choose the path of least resistance."
Dr. Bak Nguyen

0013
FROM INDUSTRIES' DISRUPTORS
"Be mindful of the consequences."
Dr. Bak Nguyen

0014
FROM CHANGING THE WORLD FROM A DENTAL CHAIR
"Hammering air three times over and
it will become steel."
Dr. Bak Nguyen

0015

"Mdex, for joy for life."

Dr. Bak Nguyen

0016

"Confidence is sexy."

Dr. Bak Nguyen

0017

"Make it happen!"

Dr. Bak Nguyen

0018

"Humility is to know what you are and to recognize what you are not."

Dr. Bak Nguyen

0019

"On thin ice, speed up, that's how you will eventually learn to fly! "

Dr. Bak Nguyen

0020

FROM MOMENTUM TRANSFER

"Control with wisdom is called influence."

Dr. Bak Nguyen

0021

FROM MOMENTUM TRANSFER

"To stabilize a momentum, speed up!"

Dr. Bak Nguyen

0022

FROM HYBRID

"Chords and patterns are the themes of the Universe."

Dr. Bak Nguyen

0023

FROM HYBRID

"A weakness is a strength out of reach."

Dr. Bak Nguyen

0024

FROM HYBRID

"Look for your next immediate win."

Dr. Bak Nguyen

0025
FROM REBOOT, TO GROW FROM MIDLIFE CRISIS
"Don't stop the flow of a river unless you are ready to clean up the flood."
Dr. Bak Nguyen

0026
FROM LEVERAGE COMMUNICATION INTO SUCCESS
"Find your worth in the service of others."
Dr. Bak Nguyen

0027
FROM LEVERAGE COMMUNICATION INTO SUCCESS
"Humility is not the denial of oneself but the acceptance of one true nature."
Dr. Bak Nguyen

0028
FROM THE BOOK OF LEGENDS, VOLUME 1
"We are all born little, as a chicken heart. If we keep an open mind, we will grow into a lion heart. Some will choose to be close-minded and will remain small."
Dr. Bak Nguyen

0029
FROM THE BOOK OF LEGENDS, VOLUME 1
"To have an open mind is step one.
To keep growing, one needs an open heart."
Dr. Bak Nguyen

0030
FROM THE BOOK OF LEGENDS, VOLUME 1
"Humility is the ability to recognize and to respect
what we are, and stop pretending to be
what we are not."
Dr. Bak Nguyen

0031
FROM SELFMADE
"Good things start to happen when you say yes!"
Dr. Bak Nguyen

0032
FROM SELFMADE
"Knowledge is the ground of the past.
Hope and Dreams are the air of the future."
Dr. Bak Nguyen

0033
FROM SELFMADE
"My deepest fear is to show up before God
and not have enough to show for."
Dr. Bak Nguyen

0034

"To make the world a better place."

Dr. Bak Nguyen

0035

FROM THE RISE OF THE UNICORN

"A Momentum is when it is easier
to keep moving than to stop."

Dr. Bak Nguyen

0036

FROM CHAMPION MINDSET

"I was open, and I bet on myself."

Dr. Bak Nguyen

0037

FROM HOW TO WRITE A BOOK IN 30 DAYS

"To keep Momentum, aim for the next win,
as little as it might be."

Dr. Bak Nguyen

0038

FROM HOW TO WRITE A BOOK IN 30 DAYS

"A quote is a truth from another life,
from a past legacy."

Dr. Bak Nguyen

0039
FROM HOW TO WRITE A BOOK IN 30 DAYS
"The fewer the words, the better."
Dr. Bak Nguyen

0040
FROM POWER, EMOTIONAL INTELLIGENCE
"Align your emotions and your ambitions
to be whole, to be unstoppable."
Dr. Bak Nguyen

0041
FROM POWER, EMOTIONAL INTELLIGENCE
"I believe in myself, and I do it for God,
not the other way around."
Dr. Bak Nguyen

0042
FROM BRANDING
"I kept the "Dr." on to remind me to always
put your interests before mine."
Dr. Bak Nguyen

0043
FROM BRANDING
"Arrogance is not the bragging of our knowledge,
but rather the denial of our ignorance."
Dr. Bak Nguyen

0044

FROM HORIZON VOLUME ONE

"I treat people, not teeth."

Dr. Bak Nguyen

0045

FROM THE POWER OF YES, VOLUME 1

"Writing books allowed me to evolve
at the speed of my thoughts."

Dr. Bak Nguyen

0046

FROM THE POWER OF YES, VOLUME 1

"Speed is my power. Momentum, my expression."

Dr. Bak Nguyen

0047

FROM THE POWER OF YES VOLUME 3

"We do not need to choose, only to prioritize."

Dr. Bak Nguyen

0048

FROM HOW TO NOT FAIL AS A DENTIST

"Changing the world from a dental chair."

Dr. Bak Nguyen

0049
FROM HOW TO NOT FAIL AS A DENTIST
"I am not giving up, I am simply wising up!"

Dr. Bak Nguyen

0050
FROM HOW TO NOT FAIL AS A DENTIST
"With your money, do not trust anyone but yourself."

Dr. Bak Nguyen

0051
FROM HUMILITY FOR SUCCESS
"Reading will be cool again!"

Dr. Bak Nguyen

0052
FROM HUMILITY FOR SUCCESS
"Until it is done, it is air, good air but only air."

Dr. Bak Nguyen

0053
FROM MASTERMIND
"You can cheat, legally, by learning about shortcuts and leveraging."

Dr. Bak Nguyen

0054

FROM PLAYBOOK INTRODUCTION VOLUME 1

"Nothing will last forever, and nothing is free."

Dr. Bak Nguyen

0055

FROM PLAYBOOK INTRODUCTION VOLUME 2

"Be careful since doubts is a pet
that you are feeding."

Dr. Bak Nguyen

0056

FROM PLAYBOOK INTRODUCTION VOLUME 2

"Reach for your next win as soon as possible,
and build on it!"

Dr. Bak Nguyen

0057

FROM AMONGST THE ALPHAS, VOLUME 2

"Be bold, confident, and humble."

Dr. Bak Nguyen

0058

FROM AMONGST THE ALPHAS, VOLUME 2

"Growth happens at the giving end,
not the receiving one."

Dr. Bak Nguyen

0059
FROM SUCCESS IS A CHOICE
"Be bold, be flexible, act fast and stay humble."
Dr. Bak Nguyen

0060
FROM SUCCESS IS A CHOICE
"To succeed, be flexible."
Dr. Bak Nguyen

0061
FROM 90 DAYS CHALLENGE
"In times of crisis, one has to reinvent oneself."
Dr. Bak Nguyen

0062
FROM RISING
"To matter, serve."
Dr. Bak Nguyen

0063
FROM RISING
"There is no free money."
Dr. Bak Nguyen

0064
FROM AFTERMATH
"For the first time of our lifetime,
all the interests of the world are aligned."
Dr. Bak Nguyen

0065

FROM AFTERMATH

"In times of crisis, it is the perfect opportunity
to reinvent who we are. "

Dr. Bak Nguyen

0066

FROM AFTERMATH

"Yes, we can have it all!"

Dr. Bak Nguyen

0067

FROM TORNADO

"History will say that to celebrate one world record,
we scored two more!"

Dr. Bak Nguyen

0068

FROM TORNADO

"The only way to keep overdelivering
is playing, all-in!"

Dr. Bak Nguyen

0069

FROM TORNADO

"Dream and the means will come."

Dr. Bak Nguyen

0070

FROM ALPHA LADDERS VOLUME ONE

"All good things start with a YES."

Dr. Bak Nguyen

0071

FROM ALPHA LADDERS VOLUME 2

"Growth occurs at the giving end, always."

Dr. Bak Nguyen

0072

FROM THE CONFESSION OF AN OVERACHIEVER

"Being lazy doesn't mean that you don't have to do shit, it means that you don't have to go through shit to get things done."

Dr. Bak Nguyen

0073

FROM TO OVERACHIEVE EVERYTHING BEING LAZY

"Arrogance is not the recognition of who we are but the denial of what we are not."

Dr. Bak Nguyen

0074

FROM TO OVERACHIEVE EVERYTHING BEING LAZY

"You call me doctor to remind me to always put your needs before mine."

Dr. Bak Nguyen

0075

FROM TO OVERACHIEVE EVERYTHING BEING LAZY

"Nowadays, influence is power without liability."

Dr. Bak Nguyen

0076

FROM TO OVERACHIEVE EVERYTHING BEING LAZY

"I told you that everything in life is a trade.
Be careful of what you are trading."

Dr. Bak Nguyen

0077

FROM SHORTCUT VOLUME 1 - HEALING

"Fear is a disease and it must be treated like one."

Dr. Bak Nguyen

This is **Shortcut volume 7, Happiness**. Welcome to the Alphas.

Dr. BAK NGUYEN

CONCLUSION

by Dr. BAK NGUYEN

We are at the end of a journey together. When one journey ends, a new one has already started a little while ago. Your personal awakening, if not already well on the way, started at the doctor's chapter. You stayed with me to know more and to be prepared before the big jump.

Well, guess what? You don't have to jump, you already did. That bridge was this journey. Now you are in power and in momentum to run to your Destiny, to complete your healing, to further your growth, and to ascend. Once you will be out of these journeys, your will be writing your own legend, rising.

And to us, white coats, we have all the attributes and habits to do so already. With our training and discipline, with our mindset, we are prepared to perform and to endure. Stop enduring the lies and the fights, and start performing your rise.

Find yourself, make peace and empower your voice and emotions. This is not a revolution, this is not a fight, it is an awakening and the end of the **age of denials**.

People talk about the age of innocence as we were younger and untouched by Conformity yet. Well,

Conformity followed. This is your cue to awake and to find your place in, not the world but the Universe.

To me, it turned out that I have made complete peace with my past and regrets. I am still a doctor but now, a happier one, a powerful one as I turned my attention to the future of the profession. Until my awakening, I was aiming to be the best, to be better than the average.

Now, my goal is to help others to emerge and to rise, to do better than me. I will keep be running ahead but now, I welcome those with the capability to surpass me. I have applied that mindset and philosophy with my colleagues and peers, not just from Mdex, but from around the world.

On a personal note, I am healed and rising. Before I help people improving their confidence through their smiles. Today, even if I keep practicing, I know that I will be helping more and more people gain confidence from their awakening, healing, and growth.

Have I changed? Yes and no. The doctor in me is still healing people and empowering their confidence. In my rise, I have transcended the teeth and smiles for the mind and entire body. I am doing this out of my free will and happy to do so because I finally found my voice and my place in the Universe.

And this is my hope to each and every one of you, white coats, doctors. With your healing and growth, you will have more power and tools to heal the world with, to bring warmth, and to restore hope to the world.

You will keep fighting the viruses and the illness but now your reward will be of a different scope, one much bigger, as you are restoring the life forces of the universe. Talking about good deeds, you have no minor role to play in the future of our kind, of humankind.

You don't have to tell them what to do, you have already inspired them to best, by being whole, being happy, and above all, by being kind and secure.

I am sure that this is already how all of you are practicing medicine on a daily basis… Now that you have awoken, you can now see the hope you are healing the world with. Embrace that energy and grow from it. Growth occurs at the giving end, and giving, that you know very well.

If this journey is the conclusion of a journey and of the **dragon walk** to me (8 books), it does not have to be for you. Those who feel ready to heal, by all means, I wish you luck.

For those who need to understand more, I invite you to pick up the **SHORTCUT** volumes from the beginning, starting with healing in volume 1.

If you were looking for a cheat, the first 3 volumes are a must, explaining the process of the awakening from **HEALING** to **GROWTH** to **RISING**.

The most important volume of **RISING** is **LEADERSHIP** to keep rising with no or less resistance. Volume 4, 5, 6, and 7 are all part of the **RISING series**, both will cover different aspects in depth. Volume 8, **DOCTOR** is a special one, one to honour my past and legacy as a doctor, of how I healed and rose.

Actually, it was the last volume of the series both it can also be a prequel, this is how and when I started to heal and to awake. I discovered the mapping and the mindset through the glasses of a doctor and a white coat.

So what you feel, I felt too. What you will face ahead, I've been there, may in a different light, but I been there too and I can tell you the outcome and the alternatives.

Rising, you will finally break through the **GLASS CEILING** from the Pyramid of Maslow, going above belonging to reconcile with yourself.

That's your **Quest of Identity**, a journey you must do alone. Well, even if have to walk that one alone, it does not have to be lonely. And that is where we met.

My brothers and sisters in arms, white coats, doctors, I thank you for your service and continuous dedication to our world. This time, it is your turn to heal and to replenish.

Enjoy that personal time and take as long as you need travelling the journey of awakening, of Identity. Be ready for more, much more, and for better. Once you are ready and whole, the rise of your legend is next.

This is **Shortcut volume 8, Doctor**. Welcome to the Alphas.

Dr. BAK NGUYEN

ANNEX

GLOSSARY OF Dr. BAK's LIBRARY

1

REINVENT YOURSELF FROM ANY CRISIS

BY Dr. BAK NGUYEN

In 1SELF is about to reinvent yourself to rise from any crisis. Written in the midst of the COVID war, now more than ever, we need hope and the know-how to bridge the future. More than just the journey of Dr. Bak, this time, Dr. Bak is sharing his journey with mentors and people who built part of the world as we know it. Interviewed in this book, CHRISTIAN TRUDEAU, former CEO and FOUNDER of BCE EMERGIS (BELL CANADA), he also digitalized the Montreal Stock Exchange.RON KLEIN, American Innovator, inventor of the magnetic stripe of the credit card, of MLS (Multi-listing services) and the man who digitalized WALL STREET bonds markets.ANDRE CHATELAIN, former first vice-president of the MOVEMENT DESJARDINS. Dr. JEAN DE SERRES, former CEO of HEMA QUEBEC. These men created billions in values and have changed our lives, even without us knowing. They all come together to share their experiences and knowledge to empower each and everyone to emerge stronger from this crisis, from any crisis.

A

BUSINESS AFTER THE GREAT PAUSE

BY Dr. BAK NGUYEN & Dr. ERIC LACOSTE

In AFTERMATH, Dr. Bak joins forces with Community leader and philanthrope Dr. Eric Lacoste. Two powerful minds and forces of nature in the reaction to the worst economic meltdown in modern times. We are all victims of the CORONA virus. Both just like humans have learned to adapt to survive, so is our economy. Most business structures and management philosophies are inherited from the age of industrialization and beyond. COVID-19 has shot down the world economy with months. At the time of the AFTERMATH, the truth is many corporations and organizations will either have to upgrade to the INFORMATION AGE or disappear. More than the INFORMATION upgrade, the era of SOCIAL MEDIA and the MILLENNIALS are driving a revolution in the core philosophy of all organizations. Profit is not king anymore, support is. In this time and age where a teenager with a social account can compete with the million dollars PR firm, social implication is now the new cornerstone. Those who will adapt will prevail and prosper, while the resistance and old guards will soon be forgotten as fossils of a past era.

ALPHA LADDERS -075
CAPTAIN OF YOUR DESTINY
BY Dr. BAK NGUYEN & JONAS DIOP

In ALPHA LADDERS, Dr. Bak is sharing his private conversation and board meetings with 2 of his trusted lieutenants, strategist Jonas Diop and international Counsellor, Brenda Garcia. As both the Dr. Bak and ALPHA brands are gaining in popularity and traction, it was time to get the movement to the next level. Now, it's about building a community and to help everyone willing to become ALPHAS to find their powers. Dr. Bak is a natural recruiter of ALPHAS and peers. He also spent the last 20 years plus, training and mentoring proteges. Now comes the time to empower more and more proteges to become ALPHAS. ALPHAS LADDERS is the journey of how Dr. Bak went from a product of Conformity to rise into a force of Nature, know as a kind tornado. In ALPHA LADDERS Jonas pushed Dr. Bak to retrace each of the steps of his awakening, steps that we can breakdown and reproduce for ourselves. The goal is to empower each willing individual to become the ultimate Captain of his or her destiny, and to do it, again and again. Welcome to the Alphas.

ALPHA LADDERS 2 -081
SHAPING LEADERS AND ACHIEVERS
BY Dr. BAK NGUYEN & BRENDA GARCIA

In ALPHA LADDERS 2, Dr. Bak is sharing the second part of his private conversation and board meetings with his trusted lieutenants. This time it is with international Counsellor, Brenda Garcia that the dialogue is taking place. In this second tome, the journey is taken to the next level. If the first tome was about the WHYs and the HOWs at an individual level, this tome is about the WHYs and the HOWs at the societal level. Through the lens of her background in international relations and diplomacy, Brenda now has the mission to help Dr. Bak establish structures, not only for his emerging organization and legacy, THE ALPHAS, but to also inspire all the other leaders and structures of our society. To do this, Brenda is taking Dr. Bak on an anthropological, sociological and philosophical journey to revisit different historical key moments in various fields and eras, going as far back as in ancient Greece at the dawn of democracy, all the way to the golden era of modern multilateralism embodied by the UN structure. Learning from the legacies of prominent figures going from Plato to Ban Ki Moon, Martin Luther King or Nelson Mandela, to Machiavelli, Marx and Simone de Beauvoir, Brenda and Dr. Bak are attempting to grasp the essence of structure and hierarchy, their goal being to empower each willing individual to become the ultimate Captain of their own success, to climb up the ladders no matter how high it is, and to build their legacy one step at a time.

AMONGST THE ALPHAS -058
BY Dr. BAK NGUYEN, with Dr. MARIA KUNDSTATER, Dr. PAUL OUELLETTE and Dr. JEREMY KRELL

In AMONGST THE ALPHAS Dr. Bak opens the blueprint of the next level with the hope that everyone can be better, bigger, wiser, but above all, a philosophy of Life that if, well applied, can bring inspiration to life. The Alphas rose in the midst of the COVID war as an International Collaboration to empower individuals to rise from the global crisis. Joining Dr. Bak are some of the world thinkers and achievers, the Alphas. Doctors, business people, thinkers, achievers, influencers, they are coming together to define what is an Alpha and his or her role, making the world a better place. This isn't the American dream, it is the human dream, one that can help you make History.Joining Dr. Bak are 3 Alpha authors, Dr. Maria Kundstater, Dr. Paul Ouellette and Dr. Jeremy Krell. This book started with questions from coach Jonas Diop. Welcome to the Alphas.

AMONGST THE ALPHAS vol.2 -059
ON THE OTHER SIDE
BY Dr. BAK NGUYEN with Dr. JULIO REYNAFARJE, Dr. LINA DUSEVICIUTE and Dr. DUC-MINH LAM-DO

In AMONGST THE ALPHAS 2, Dr. Bak continues to explore the meaning of what it is to be an Alpha and how to act amongst Alphas, because as the saying taught us: alone one goes fast, together we goes far. Some people see the problem. Some people look at the problem, some people created the problem. Some people leverage the problem into solutions and opportunities. Well, all of those people are Alphas. Networking and leveraging one another, their powers and reach are beyond measure. And one will keep the other in line too. Joining Dr. Bak are 3 Alphas from around the world coming together to share and collaborate, Dr. DUSEVICIUTE, Dr. LAM-DO and Dr. REYNAFARJE. This isn't the American dream, it is the human dream, one that can help you make History. Welcome to the Alphas.

B

BOOTCAMP -071
BOOKS TO REWRITE MINDSETS INTO WINNING STATES OF MIND
BY Dr. BAK NGUYEN

In BOOTCAMP 8 BOOKS TO REWRITE MINDSETS INTO WINNING STATES OF MIND, Dr. Bak is taking you into his past, before the visionary entrepreneur, before the world records, before the Industry's disruptor status. Here are 8 of the books that changed Dr. Bak's thinking and, therefore, reset his evolution into the course we now know him for. BOOTCAMP: 8 BOOKS TO REWRITE MINDSETS INTO WINNING STATES OF MIND, is a Bootcamp of 8 weeks for anyone looking to experience Dr. Bak's training to become THE Dr. BAK you came to know and love. This book will summarize how each title changed Dr. Bak mindset into a state of mind and how he applied that to rewrite his destiny. 8 books to read, that's 8 weeks of Bootcamp to access the power of your MIND and of your WILL. Are you ready for a change?

BRANDING -044
BALANCING STRATEGY AND EMOTIONS
BY Dr. BAK NGUYEN

BRANDING is communication to its most powerful state. Branding is not just about communicating anymore but about making a promise, about establishing a relation, about generating an emotion. More than once, Dr. Bak proved himself to be a master, communicating and branding his ideas into flags attracting interest and influences, nationally and internationally. In BRANDING, Dr. Bak shares a very unique and personal journey, branding Dr. Bak. How does he go from Dr. Nguyen, a loved and respected dentist to becoming Dr. Bak, a world anchor hosting THE ALPHAS in the medical and financial world?More than a personal journey, BRANDING helps to break down the steps to elevate someone with nothing else but the force of his or her spirit. Welcome to the Alphas.

C

CHANGING THE WORLD FROM A DENTAL CHAIR -007
BY Dr. BAK NGUYEN

Since he has received the EY's nomination for entrepreneur of the year for his startup Mdex & Co, Dr. Bak Nguyen has pushed the opportunity to the next level. Speaker, author, and businessman, Dr. Bak is a true entrepreneur and industries' disruptor. To compensate for the startup's status of Mdex & Co, he challenged himself to write a book based on the EY's questionnaire to share an in-depth vision of his company. With "Changing the World from a dental chair" Dr. Bak is sharing his thought process and philosophy to his approach to the industry. Not looking to revolutionize but rather to empower, he became, despite himself, an industries disruptor: an entrepreneur who has established a new benchmark. Dr. Bak Nguyen is a cosmetic dentist and visionary businessman who won the GRAND HOMAGE prize of "LYS de la Diversité" 2016, for his contribution as a citizen and entrepreneur in the community. He also holds recognitions from the Canadian Parliament and the Canadian Senate.

In 2003, he founded Mdex, a dental company upon which in 2018, he launched the most ambitious private endeavour to reform the dental industry, Canada wide. He wrote seven books covering ENTREPRENEURSHIP, LEADERSHIP, QUEST of IDENTITY, and now, PROFESSION HEALTH. Philosopher, he has close to his heart the quest of happiness of the people surrounding him, patients, and colleagues alike. Those projects have allowed Dr. Nguyen to attract interests from the international and diplomatic community and he is now the centre of a global discussion on the wellbeing and the future of the health profession. It is in that matter that he shares with you his thoughts and encourages the health community to share their own stories.

CHAMPION MINDSET -039
LEARNING TO WIN
BY Dr. BAK NGUYEN & CHRISTOPHE MULUMBA

CHAMPION MINDSET is the encounter of the business world and the professional sports world. Industries' Disruptor Dr. BAK NGUYEN shares his wisdom and views with the HAMMER, CFL Football Star, Edmonton's Eskimos CHRISTOPHE MULUMBA on how to leverage on the champion mindset to create successful entrepreneurs. Writing and challenging each other, they discovered the parallels and the difference of both worlds, but mainly, the recipe for leveraging from one to succeed in the other, from champions and entrepreneurs to WINNERS. Build and score your millions, it is a matter of mindset! This is CHAMPION MINDSET.

E

EMPOWERMENT -069
BY Dr. BAK NGUYEN

In EMPOWERMENT, Dr. Bak's 69th book, writing a book every 8 days for 8 weeks in a row to write the next world record of writing 72 books/36 months, Dr. Bak is taking a rest, sharing his inner feelings, inspiration, and motivation. Much more than his diary, EMPOWERMENT is the key to walk in his footsteps and to comprehend the process of an overachiever. Dr. Bak's helped and inspired countless people to find their voice, to live their dream, and to be the better version of themselves. Why is he sharing as much and keep sharing? Why is he going that fast, always further and further, why and how is he keeping his inspiration and momentum? Those are all the answers EMPOWERMENT will deliver to you. This book might be one of the fastest Dr. Bak has written, not because of time constraints but from inspiration, pure inspiration to share and to grow. There is always a dark side to each power, two faces to a coin. Well, this is the less prominent facets of Dr. Bak Momentum and success, the road to his MINDSET.

F

FORCES OF NATURE -015
FORGING THE CHARACTER OF WINNERS
BY Dr. BAK NGUYEN

In FORCES OF NATURE, Dr. Bak is giving his all. This is his 15 books written within 15 months. It is the end of a marathon to set the next world record. For the occasion, he wanted to end with a big bang! How about a book with all of his biggest challenges? A Quest of Identity, a journey looking for his name and powers, Dr. Bak is borrowing with myths and legends to make this journey universal. Yes, this is Dr. Bak's mythology. Demons, heroes and Gods, there are forces of Nature that we all meet on our way for our name. Some will scare us, some will fight us, some will manipulate us. We can flee, we can hide, we can fight. What we do will define our next encounter and the one after. A tale of personal growth, a journey to find power and purpose, Dr. Bak is showing us the path to freedom, the Path of Life. Welcome to the Alphas.

H

HORIZON, BUILDING UP THE VISION -045
VOLUME ONE
BY Dr. BAK NGUYEN

Dr. Bak is opening up at your demand! Many of you are following Dr. Bak online and are asking to know more about his lifestyle. This is how he has chosen to respond: sharing his lifestyle as he traveled the world and what he learned in each city to come to build his Mindset as a driver and a winner. Here are 10 destinations (over 69

160

that will be following in the next volumes...) in which he shares his journey. New York, Quebec, Paris, Punta Cana, Monaco, Los Angeles, Nice, Holguin, the journey happened over twenty years.

HORIZON, ON THE FOOTSTEP OF TITANS -048
VOLUME TWO
BY Dr. BAK NGUYEN

Dr. Bak is opening up at your demand! Many of you are following Dr. Bak online and are asking to know more about his lifestyle. This is how he has chosen to respond: sharing his lifestyle as he traveled the world and what he learned in each city to come to build his Mindset as a driver and a winner. Here are 9 destinations (over 72 that will be following in the next volumes...) in which he shares his journey. Hong Kong, London, Rome, San Francisco, Anaheim, and more..., the journey happened over twenty years. Dr. Bak is sharing with you his feelings, impressions, and how they shaped his state of mind and character into Dr. Bak. From a dreamer to a driver and a builder, the journey started since he was 3. Wealth is a state of mind, and a state of mind is the basis of the drive. Find out about the mind of an Industry's disruptor.

HORIZON, DREAMING OF THE FUTURE -068
VOLUME THREE
BY Dr. BAK NGUYEN

Dr. Bak is back. From the midst of confinement, he remembers and writes about what life was, when traveling was a natural part of Life. It will come back. Now more than ever, we need to open both our hearts and minds to fight fear and intolerance. Writing from a time of crisis, he is sharing the magic and psychological effect of seeing the world and how it has shaped his mindset. Here are 9 other destinations (over 75) in which he shares his journey. Beijing, Key West, Madrid, Amsterdam, Marrakech and more..., the journey happened over twenty years.

HOW TO NOT FAIL AS A DENTIST -047
BY Dr. BAK NGUYEN

In HOW TO NOT FAIL AS A DENTIST, Dr. Bak is given 20 plus years of experience and knowledge of what it is to be a dentist on the ground. PROFESSIONAL INTELLIGENCE, FINANCIAL INTELLIGENCE and MANAGEMENT INTELLIGENCE are the fields that any dentist will have to master for a chance to success and a shot for happiness practicing dentistry. Where ever you are starting your career as a new graduate or a veteran in the field looking to reach the next level, this is book smart and street smart all into one. This is Million Dollar Mindset applied to dentistry. We won't be making a millionaire out of you from this book, we will be giving you a shot to happiness and success. The million will follow soon enough.

HOW TO WRITE A BOOK IN 30 DAYS -042
BY Dr. BAK NGUYEN

In HOW TO WRITE YOUR BOOK IN 30 DAYS, Dr. Bak has crafted writing skills and techniques that can be shared and mastered. This book is mainly about structure and how to keep moving forward, avoiding the hit of the INSPIRATION WALL. You will find a wealth of wisdom from his experience writing your first, second, or even 10th book. Dr. Bak is sharing his secrets writing books, having written himself 72 books within 36 months. Visionary businessman, doctor in dentistry, Dr. Bak describes himself as a Dentist by circumstances, a communicator by passion, and an entrepreneur by nature.

HOW TO WRITE A SUCCESSFUL BUSINESS PLAN -049
BY Dr. BAK NGUYEN & ROUBA SAKR

In HOW TO WRITE A SUCCESSFUL BUSINESS PLAN, Dr. Bak is given 20 plus years of experience and knowledge of what it is to be an entrepreneur and more importantly, how to have the investors and banks on your side. Being an entrepreneur is surely not something you learn from school, but there are steps to master so you can communicate your views and vision. That's the only way you will have financing.Writing a business is only not a mandatory stop only for the bankers, but an essential step to every entrepreneur, to know the direction and what's coming next. A business plan is also not set in stone, if there is a truth in business is that nothing will go as planned. Writing down your business plan the first time will prepare you to adapt and to overcome the challenges and surprises. For most entrepreneurs, a business is a passion. To most investors and all banks, a business is a system. Your business plan is the map to that system. However unique your ideas and business are, the mapping follows the same steps and pattern.

HUMILITY FOR SUCCESS -051
BALANCING STRATEGY AND EMOTIONS
BY Dr. BAK NGUYEN

HUMILITY FOR SUCCESS is exploring the emotional discomforts and challenges champions, and overachievers put themselves through. Success is never done overnight and on the way, just like the pain and the struggles aren't enough, we are dealing with the doubts, the haters, and those who like to tell us how to live our lives and what to do. At the same time, nothing of worth can be achieved alone. Every legend has a cast of characters, allies, mentors, companions, rivals, and foes. So one needs the key to social behaviour. HUMILITY FOR SUCCESS is exploring the matter and will help you sort out beliefs from values, peers from friends. Humility is much more about how we see ourselves than how others see us. For any entrepreneur and champion, our daily is to set our mindset right, and to perfect our skills, not to fit in. There is a world where CONFIDENCE grows is in synergy with HUMILITY. As you set the right label on the right belief, you will be able to grow and to leave the lies and haters far behinds. This is HUMILITY FOR SUCCESS.

HYBRID -011
THE MODERN QUEST OF IDENTITY
BY Dr. BAK NGUYEN

IDENTITY -004
THE ANTHOLOGY OF QUESTS
BY Dr. BAK NGUYEN

What if John Lennon was still alive and running for president today? What kind of campaign will he be running? IDENTIFY -THE ANTHOLOGY OF QUESTS is about the quest each of us has to undertake, sooner or later, THE QUEST OF IDENTITY. Citizen of the world, aim to be one, the one, one whole, one unity, made of many. That's the anthology of life! Start with your one, find your unity, and your legend will start. We are all small-minded people anyway! We need each other to be one! We need each other to be happy, so we, so you, so I, can be happy. This is the chorus of life. This is our song! Citizens of the world, I salute you! This is the first tome of the IDENTITY QUEST. FORCES OF NATURE (tome 2) will be following in SUMMER 2021. Also under development, Tome 3 - THE CONQUEROR WITHIN will start production soon.

INDUSTRIES DISRUPTORS -006
BY Dr. BAK NGUYEN

INDUSTRIES DISRUPTORS is a strange title, one that sparkles mixed feelings. A disruptor is someone making a difference, and since we, in general, do not like change, the label is mostly negative. But a disruptor is mostly someone who sees the same problem and challenge from another angle. The disruptor will tackle that angle and come up with something new from something existent. That's evolution! In INDUSTRIES DISRUPTORS, Dr. Bak is joining forces with James Stephan-Usypchuk to share with us what is going on in the minds and shoes of those entrepreneurs disrupting the old habits. Dr. Bak is changing the world from a dental chair, disrupting the dental, and now the book industry. James is a maverick in the Intelligence space, from marketing to Artificial Intelligence. Coming from very different backgrounds and industries, they end up telling very similar stories. If disruptors change the world, well, their story proves that disruptors can be made and forged. Here's the recipe. Here are their stories.

K

KRYPTO -040
TO SAVE THE WORLD
BY Dr. BAK NGUYEN & ILYAS BAKOUCH

L

LEADERSHIP -003
PANDORA'S BOX
BY Dr. BAK NGUYEN

LEADERSHIP, PANDORA'S BOX is 21 presidential speeches for a better tomorrow for all of us. It aims to drive HOPE and motivation into each and every one of us. Together we can make the difference, we hold such power. Covering themes from LOYALTY to GENEROSITY, from FREEDOM and INTELLIGENCE to DOUBTS and DEATH, this is not the typical presidential or motivational speeches that we are used to. LEADERSHIP PANDORA'S BOX will surf your emotions first, only to dive with you to touch the core and soul of our meaning: to matter. This is not a Quest of Identity, but the cry to rally as a species, to raise our heads toward the future, and to move forward as a WHOLE. Not a typical Dr. Bak's book, LEADERSHIP, PANDORA'S BOX is a must-read for all of you looking for hope and purpose, all of us, citizens of the world.

LEVERAGE -014
COMMUNICATION INTO SUCCESS
BY Dr. BAK NGUYEN

In LEVERAGE COMMUNICATION TO SUCCESS, Dr. Bak shares his secret and mindsets to elevate an idea into a vision and a vision into an endeavour. Some endeavours will be a project, some others will become companies, and some will grow into a movement. It does not matter, each started with great communication.Communication is a very vast concept, education, sale, sharing, empowering, coaching, preaching, entertaining. Those are all different kinds of communication. The intent differs, the audiences vary, the messages are unique but the frame can be templated and mastered. In LEVERAGE COMMUNICATION TO SUCCESS, Dr. Bak is loyal to his core, sharing only what he knows best, what he has done himself. This book is dedicated to communicating successfully in business.

M

MASTERMIND, 7 WAYS INTO THE BIG LEAGUE -052
BY Dr. BAK NGUYEN & JONAS DIOP

MASTERMIND, 7 WAYS INTO THE BIG LEAGUE is the result of the encounter of business coach Jonas Diop and Dr. Bak. As a professional podcaster and someone always seeking the truth and ways to leverage success and performance, coach Jonas is putting Dr. Bak to the test, one that should reveal his secret to overachieve month after month, accumulating a new world record every month. Follow those two great minds as they push each other to surpass themselves, each in their own way and own style. MASTERMIND, 7 WAYS INTO THE BIG LEAGUE is more than a roadmap to success, it is a journey and a live testimony as you are turning the pages, one by one.

MIDAS TOUCH -065
POST-COVID DENTISTRY
BY Dr. BAK NGUYEN, Dr. JULIO REYNAFARJE AND Dr. PAUL OUELLETTE

MIDAS TOUCH, is the memoir of what happened in the ALPHAS SUMMIT in the midst of the GREAT PAUSE as great minds throughout the world in the dental field are coming together. As the time of competition is obsolete, the new era of collaboration is blooming. This is the 3rd book of the ALPHAS, after AFTERMATH and RELEVANCY, all written in the midst of confinement. Dr. Julio Reynafarje is bearing this initiative, to share with you the secret of a successful and lasting relationship with your patients, balancing science and psychology, kindness, and professionalism. He personally invited the ALPHAS to join as co-author, Dr. Paul Ouellette, and Dr.

Paul Dominique, and Dr. Bak.Together, they have more than 100 years of combined experience, wisdom, trade, skills, philosophy, and secrets to share with you to empower you in the rebuilding of the dental profession in the aftermath of COVID. RELEVANCY was about coming together and to rebuild the future. MIDAS TOUCH is about how to build, one treatment plan at a time, one story at a time, one smile at a time.

MINDSET ARMORY -050
BY Dr. BAK NGUYEN

MINDSET ARMORY is Dr. Bak's 49th book, days after he completed his world record of writing 48 books within 24 months, on top of being a CEO of Mdex & Co and a full-time cosmetic dentist. Dr. Bak is undoubtedly an OVERACHIEVER. From his last books, he has shared more and more of his lifestyle and how it forged his winning mindset. Within MINDSET ARMORY, Dr. Bak is sharing with us his tools, how he found them, forged them, and leverage them. Just like any warrior needs a shield, a sword, and a ride, here are Dr. Bak's. For any entrepreneur, the road to success is a long and winding journey. On the way, some will find allies and foes. Some allies will become foes, and some foes might become allies. In today's competitive world, the only constant is change. With the right tool, it is possible to achieve. The right tool, the right mindset. This is MINDSET ARMORY.

MIRROR -085
BY Dr. BAK NGUYEN

MIRROR is the theme for a personal book. Not only to Dr. Bak but to all of us looking to reach beyond who and what we actually are. MIRROR is special in the fact that it is not only the content of the book that is of worth but the process in which Dr. Bak shared his own evolution. To go beyond who we are, one must grow every day. And how do you compare your growth and how far have you reach? Looking in the mirror. In all of Dr. Bak's writing, looking at the past is a trap to avoid at all costs. Looking in the mirror, is that any better? Share Dr. Bak's way to push and keep pushing himself without friction nor resistance. Please read that again. To evolve without friction or resistance... that is the source of infinite growth and the unification of the Quest for Power and the Quest of Happiness.

MOMENTUM TRANSFER -009
BY Dr. BAK NGUYEN & Coach DINO MASSON

How to be successful in your business and in your life? Achieve Your Biggest Goals With MOMENTUM TRANSFER. START THE BUSINESS YOU WANT - AND BRING IT NEXT LEVEL! GET THE LIFE YOU ALWAYS WANTED - AND IMPROVE IT! TAKE ANY PROJECTS YOU HAVE - AND MAKE IT THE BEST! In this powerful book, you'll discover what a small business owner learned from a millionaire and successful entrepreneur. He applied his mentor's principles and is explaining them in full detail in this book. The small business owner wrote the book he has always wanted to read and went from the verge of bankruptcy to quadrupling his revenues in less than 9 months and improve his personal life by increasing his energy and bring back peacefulness. Together, the millionaire and the small business owner are sharing their most valuable business and life lessons to the world. The most powerful book to increase your momentum in your business and your life introduces simple and radical life-changing concepts: Multiply your business revenues by finding the Eye of your Momentum - Increase your energy by building and feeding your own Momentum - How to increase your confidence with these simple steps - How to transfer your new powerful energy into other aspects of your business and life - How to set goals and achieve them (even crush them!)- How to always tap into an effortless and limitless force within you- And much, much more!

P

PLAYBOOK INTRODUCTION -055
BY Dr. BAK NGUYEN

In PLAYBOOK INTRODUCTION, Dr. Bak is open the door to all the newcomers and aspirant entrepreneurs who are looking at where and when to start. Based on questions of two college students wanting to know how to start their entrepreneurial journey, Dr. Bak dives into his experiences to empower the next generation, not about what they should do, but how he, Dr. Bak, would have done it today. This is an important aspect to recognize in the business world, the world has changed since the INFORMATION AGE and the advent of the millenniums into the market. Most matrix and know-how have to be adapted to today's speed and accessibility to the information. We are living at the INFORMATION AGE, this book is the precursor to the ABUNDANCE AGE, at least to those open to embrace the opportunity.

PLAYBOOK INTRODUCTION 2 -056
BY Dr. BAK NGUYEN

In PLAYBOOK INTRODUCTION 2, Dr. Bak continuing the journey to welcome the newcomers and aspirant entrepreneurs looking at where and when to start. If the first volume covers the mindset, the second is covering much more in-depth the concept of debt and leverage.This is an important aspect to recognize in the business world, the world has changed since the INFORMATION AGE and the advent of the millenniums into the market. Most matrix and know-how have to be adapted to today's speed and accessibility to the information. We are living at the INFORMATION AGE, this book is the precursor to the ABUNDANCE AGE, at least to those open to embrace the opportunity.

POWER -043
EMOTIONAL INTELLIGENCE
BY Dr. BAK NGUYEN

IN POWER, EMOTIONAL INTELLIGENCE, Dr. Bak is sharing his experiences and secrets leveraging on his EMOTIONAL INTELLIGENCE, a power we all have within. From SYMPATHY, having others opening up to you, to ACTIVE LISTENING, saving you time and energy; from EMPATHY, allowing you to predict the future to INFLUENCE, enabling you to draft the future, not to forget the power of the crowd with MOMENTUM, you are now in possession of power in tune with nature, yourself. It is a unique take on the subject to empower you to find your powers and your destiny. Visionary businessman, doctor in dentistry, Dr. Bak describes himself as a Dentist by circumstances, a communicator by passion, and an entrepreneur by nature.

167

POWERPLAY -078
HOW TO BUILD THE PERFECT TEAM
BY Dr. BAK NGUYEN

In POWERPLAY, HOW TO BUILD THE PERFECT TEAM, Dr. Bak is sharing with you his experience, perspective, and mistake traveling the journey of the entrepreneur. A serial entrepreneur himself, he started venture only with a single partner as team to build companies with a director of human resources and a board of directors. POWERPLAY is not a story, it is the HOW TO build the perfect team, knowing that perfection is a lie. So how can one build a team that will empower his or her vision? How to recruit, how to train, how to retain? Those are all legitimate questions. And all of those won't matter if the first question isn't answered: what is the reason for the team? There is the old way to hire and the new way to recruit. Yes, Human Resources is all about mindset too! This journey is one of introspection, of leadership, and a cheat sheet to build, not only the perfect team but the team that will empower your legacy to the next level.

PROFESSION HEALTH - TOME ONE -005
THE UNCONVENTIONAL QUEST OF HAPPINESS
BY Dr. BAK NGUYEN, Dr. MIRJANA SINDOLIC, Dr. ROBERT DURAND AND COLLABORATORS

Why are health professionals burning out while they give the best of themselves to heal the world? Dr. Bak aims to break the curse of isolation that health professionals face and establish a conversation to start the healing process. PROFESSION HEALTH is the basis of an ongoing discussion and will also serve as an introduction to a study lead by Professor Robert Durand, DMD, MSc Science from University of Montreal, study co-financed by Mdex and the Federal Government of Canada. Co-writers are Dr. Mirjana Sindolic, Professor Robert Durand, Dr. Jean De Serres, MD and former President of Hema Quebec, Counsel-Minister Luis Maria Kalaff Sanchez, Dr. Miguel Angel Russo, MD, Banker Anthony Siggia, Banker Kyles Yves, and more...
This is the first Tome of three, dedicated to help "WHITE COATS" to heal and to find their happiness.

R

REBOOT -012
MIDLIFE CRISIS
BY Dr. BAK NGUYEN

MidLife Crisis is a common theme to each of us as we reach the threshold. As a man, as a woman, why is it that half of the marriages end up in recall? If anything else would have half those rates of failure, the lawsuits would be raining. Where are the flaws, the traps? Love is strong and pure, why is marriage not the reflection of that? All hard to ask questions with little or no answers. Dr. Bak is sharing his reflections and findings as he reached himself the WALL OF MARRIAGE. This is a matter that affects all of our lives. It is time for some answers.

RELEVANCY - TOME TWO -064
REINVENTING OURSELVES TO SURVIVE
BY Dr. BAK NGUYEN & Dr. PAUL OUELLETTE AND COLLABORATORS

THE GREAT PAUSE was a reboot of all the systems of society. Many outdated systems will not make it back. The Dental Industry is a needed one, it has laid on complacency for far too long. In an age where expertise is global and democratized and can be replaced with technologies and artificial intelligence, the REBOOT will force, not just an update, but an operating system replacement and a firmware upgrade.First, they saved their industry with THE ALPHAS INITIATIVE, sharing their knowledge and vision freely to all the world's dental industry. With the OUELLETTE INITIATIVE, they bought some time to all the dental clinics to resume and to adjust. The warning has been given, the clock is now ticking. who will prevail and prosper and who will be left behind, outdated and obsolete?

RISING -062
TO WIN MORE THAN YOU ARE AFRAID TO LOSE
BY Dr. BAK NGUYEN

In RISING, TO WIN MORE TAN YOU ARE AFRAID TO LOSE, Dr. Bak is breaking down the strategy to success to all, not only those wearing white coats and scrubs. More than his previous book (SUCCESS IS A CHOICE), this one is covering most of the aspects of getting to the next level, psychologically, socially, and financially. Rising is broken down into three key strategies: Financial Leverage - Compressing time - Always being in control. Presented by MILLION DOLLAR MINDSET, the book is covering more than the ways to create wealth, but also how to reach happiness and to live a life without regrets. Dr. Bak the CEO and founder of Mdex & Co, a company with the promise of reforming the whole dental industry for the better. He wrote more than 60 books within 30 months as he is sharing his experiences, secrets, and wisdom.

S

SELFMADE -036
GRATITUDE AND HUMILITY
BY Dr. BAK NGUYEN

This is the story of Dr. Bak, an artist who became a dentist, a dentist who became an Entrepreneur, an Entrepreneur who is seeking to save an entire industry.In his free time, Dr. Bak managed to write 37 books and is a contender to 3 world records to be confirmed. Businessman and visionary, his views and philosophy are ahead of our time. This is his 37th book. In SELFMADE, Dr. Bak is answering the questions most entrepreneurs want to know, the HOWTO and the secret recipes, not just to succeed, but to keep going no matter what! SELFMADE is the perfect read for any entrepreneurs, novices, and veterans.

SHORTCUT vol. 1 - HEALING -093
BY Dr. BAK NGUYEN

In SHORTCUT 408 HEALING QUOTES, Dr. Bak revisits and compiles his journey of healing and growing. Just anyone, he was molded and shaped by Conformity and Society to the point of blending and melting. Walking his journey of healing, he rediscovers himself and found his true calling. And once whole with himself and with the Universe, Dr. Bak found his powers. In SHORTCUT 408 HEALING QUOTES, you have a quick and easy way to surf his mindsets and what allowed him to heal, to find back his voice and wings, and to walk his destiny. You too are walking your Quest of Identity. That one is mainly a journey of healing. May you find yours and your powers.

SHORTCUT vol. 2 - GROWING -094
BY Dr. BAK NGUYEN

In SHORTCUT 408 GROWTH QUOTES, Dr. Bak is compiling his library of books about personal growth and self-improvement. More than a motivational book, more than a compilation of knowledge, Dr. Bak is sharing the mindsets upon which he found his power to achieve and to overachieve. We all have our powers, only they were muted and forgotten as we were forged by Conformity and Society. After the healing process, walking your Quest of Identity, the Quest for you growth and God given power is next to lead you to walk your Destiny.

SHORTCUT vol. 3 - LEADERSHIP -095
BY Dr. BAK NGUYEN

In SHORTCUT 365 LEADERSHIP QUOTES, Dr. Bak is compiling his library of books about leadership and ambition. Yes, the ambition is to find your worth and to make the world a better place for all of us. If the 3rd volume of SHORTCUT is mainly a motivational compilation, it also holds the secrets and mindsets to influence and leadership. if you were looking to walk your legend and to impact the world, you are walking a lonely path.

You might on your own, but it does not have to be harder than it is. As we all have your unique challenges, the key to victory is often found in the same place, your heart. And here are 365 shortcuts to keep you believing and to attract more people to you as you are growing into a true leader.

SHORTCUT vol. 4 - CONFIDENCE 096
BY Dr. BAK NGUYEN

SHORTCUT 518 CONFIDENCE QUOTES. is the most voluminous compilation of Dr. Bak's quotes. To heal was the first step. To grow and find your powers came next. As you are walking your personal legend, Confidence is both your sword and armour to conquer your Destiny and to overcome all of the challenges on your way. In SHORTCUT volume four, Dr. Bak comprises all his mindsets and wisdom to ease your ascension. Confidence is not something one is simply born with, but something to nurture, grow, and master. Some will have the chance to be raised by people empowering Confidence, others will have to heal from Conformity to grow their confidence. It does not matter, only once Confident, can one stand tall and see clearly the horizon.

SHORTCUT vol. 5- SUCCESS 097
BY Dr. BAK NGUYEN

Success is not a destination but a journey and a side effect. While no map can lead you to success, the right mindset will forge your own success, the one without medals nor labels. If you are looking to walk your legend, to be successful is merely the beginning. Actually, being successful is often a side effect of the mindsets and actions that you took, you provoked. In SHORTCUT 317 SUCCESS QUOTES. Dr. Bak is revisiting his journey, breaking down what led him to be successful despite the odds stacked against him. As success is the consequence of mindsets, choices, and actions, it can be duplicated over and over again, one just needs to master the mindsets first.

SHORTCUT vol. 6- POWER 098
BY Dr. BAK NGUYEN

That's the kind of power that you will discover within this journey. Power is a tool, a leverage. Well used, it will lead to great achievements. Misused, it will be your downfall. If a sword sometimes has 2 edges, Power is a sword with no handle and multiple edges. You have been warned. In SHORTCUT 376 POWER QUOTES, Dr. Bak is compiling all the powers he found and mastered walking his own legend. If the first power was Confidence, very quickly, Dr. Bak realized that Confidence was the key to many, many more powers. Where to find them, how to yield them, and how to leverage these powers is the essence of the 6th volume of SHORTCUT.

SHORTCUT vol. 7- HAPPINESS 099
BY Dr. BAK NGUYEN

We were all born happy and then, somehow, we lost our ways and forgot our ways home. Is this the real tragedy behind the lost paradise myth? If we were happy once, we can trust our heart to find our way home, once more. This is the journey of the 7th volume of the SHORTCUT series. In SHORTCUT 306 HAPPINESS QUOTES, Dr. Bak is revisiting and compiling all the secrets and mindsets leading to happiness. Happiness is not just a destination but a shrine for Confidence and a safe place to regroup, to heal, to grow. We each have our own happiness. What you will learn here is where to find yours and, more importantly, how to leverage you to ease the journey ahead, because happiness is not your final destination. It can be the key to your legend.

SHORTCUT vol. 8- DOCTORS 100
BY Dr. BAK NGUYEN

If healing was the first step to your destiny and powers, there is a science to heal. Those with that science are doctors, the healers of the world. In India, healers are second only to the Gods! In SHORTCUT 170 DOCTOR QUOTES, Dr. Bak is dedicating the 8th volume of the series to his peers, doctors, from all around the world. Doctors too, have to walk their Quest of Identity, to heal from their pain and to walk their legend. Doctors need to heal and rejuvenate to keep healing the world. If healing is their science, in SHORTCUT, they will access the power of leveraging.

SUCCESS IS A CHOICE -060
BLUEPRINTS FOR HEALTH PROFESSIONALS
BY Dr. BAK NGUYEN

In SUCCESS IS A CHOICE, FINANCIAL MILLIONAIRE BLUEPRINTS FOR HEALTH PROFESSIONALS, Dr. Bak is breaking down the strategy to success for all those wearing white coats and scrubs: doctors, dentists, pharmacists, chiropractors, nurses, etc. Success is broken down into three key strategies: Financial Leverage - Compressing time - Always being in control. Presented by MILLION DOLLAR MINDSET, the book is covering more than the ways to create wealth, but also how to reach happiness and to live a life without regrets.Dr. Bak is a successful cosmetic dentist with nearly 20 years of experience. He founded Mdex & Co, a company with the promise of reforming the whole dental industry for the better. While doing so, he discovered a passion for writing and for sharing. Multiple times World Record, Dr. Bak is writing a book every 2 weeks for the last 30 months. This is his 60th book, and he is still practicing. How he does it, is what he is sharing with us, SUCCESS, HAPPINESS, and mostly FREEDOM to all Health Professionals.

SYMPHONY OF SKILLS -001
BY Dr. BAK NGUYEN

You will enlighten the world with your potential. I can't wait to see all the differences that you will have in our world. Remember that power comes with responsibility. We can feel in his presence, a genuine force, a depth of energy, confidence, innocence, courage, and intelligence. Bak is always looking for answers, morning and night, he wants to understand the why and the why not. This book is the essence of the man. Dr. Bak is a force of nature who bears proudly his title eHappy. The man never ceases smiling nor spreading his good vibe wherever he passes. He is not trapped in the nostalgia of the past nor the satisfaction of the present, he embodies the joy of what's possible, what's to come. The more we read, the more we share, and we live. That is Bak, he charms us to evolve and to share his points of view, and before we know it, we are walking by his side, a journey we never saw coming.

T

THE 90 DAYS CHALLENGE -061
BY Dr. BAK NGUYEN

THE 90 DAYS CHALLENGE, is Dr. Bak's journey into the unknown. Overachiever writing 2 books a month on average, for the last 30 months, ambitious CEO, Industries' Disruptor, Dr. Bak seems to have success in everything he touches. Everything except the control of his weight. For nearly 20 years, he struggles with an overweight problem. Every time he scored big, he added on a little more weight. Well, this time, he exposes himself out there, in real-time and without filter, accepting the challenge of his brother-in-law, DON VO to lose 45 pounds within 90 days. That's half a pound a day, for three months. He will have to do so while keeping all of his other challenges on track, writing books at a world record pace, leading the dental industry into the new ERA, and keep seeing his patients. Undoubtedly entertaining, this is the journey of an ALPHA who simply won't give up. But this time, nothing is sure.

THE BOOK OF LEGENDS -024
BY Dr. BAK NGUYEN & WILLIAM BAK

The Book of Legends vol. 1 the story behind the world record of Dr. Bak and his son, William Bak. All Dr. Bak had in mind was to keep his promise of writing a book with his son. They ended up writing 8 children's books within a month, scoring a new world record. William is also the youngest author having published in two languages. Those are world records waiting to be confirmed. History will say: to celebrate a first world record (writing 15 books / 15 months), for the love of his son, he will have scored a second world record: to write 8 books within a month! THE BOOK OF LEGENDS vol. 1 This is both a magical journey for both a father and a son looking to connect and to find themselves. Join Dr. Bak and William Bak in their journey and their love for Life!

THE BOOK OF LEGENDS 2 -041
BY Dr. BAK NGUYEN & WILLIAM BAK

THE BOOK OF LEGENDS vol. 2 is the sequel of "CINDERELLA" but a true story between a father and his son. Together they have discovered a bond and a way to connect. The first BOOK OF LEGENDS covered the time of the first four books they wrote together within a month. The second BOOK OF LEGENDS is covering what happened after the curtains dropped, what happened after reality kicked back in. If the first volume was about a fairy tale in vacation time, the second volume is about making it last in real Life. Share their journey and their love of Life!

THE BOOK OF LEGENDS 3 -086
THE END OF THE INNOCENCE AGE
BY Dr. BAK NGUYEN & WILLIAM BAK

This is the third volume of the series, THE BOOK OF LEGENDS. If the first two happened as a breeze breaking world records on top of world records (27 books written as father and son), the 3rd volume took much more time to arrive. William has grown and writing chicken books is not enough anymore to ignite his imagination. Dr. Bak, as a good father, will try to follow William's growth and invented new games, technics and mind frames to keep engaging William's imagination and interest. From auditions to backstories, Dr. Bak bent backward to keep the adventure going. More than sharing the success and the glory, within THE BOOK OF LEGENDS volume 3, you are sharing the doubts and failure of a father and son refusing to let go... but who have now left MOMENTUM... until the winds blow once more in their favour. Welcome to the Alphas.

THE CONFESSION OF A LAZY OVERACHIEVER -089
REINVENT YOURSELF FROM ANY CRISIS
BY Dr. BAK NGUYEN

In THE CONFESSION OF A LAZY OVERACHIEVER, Dr. Bak is opening up to his new marketing officer, Jamie, fresh out of school. She is young, full of energy, and looking to chill and still to have it all. True to his character, Dr. Bak is giving Jamie some leeway to redefine Dr. Bak's brand to her demographic, the Millennials. This journey is about Dr. Bak satisfying the Millennials and answering their true questions in life. A rebel himself, his ambition to change the world started back on campus, some 25 years ago... then, life caught up with him. It took Dr. Bak 20 years to shake down the burdens of life, to spread his wings free from Conformity, and to start Overachieving. Doctor, CEO, and world record author, here is what Dr. Bak would have love to know 25 years ago as was still on campus. In a word, this is cheating your way to success and freedom. And yes, it is possible. Success, Money, Freedom, it all starts with a mindset and the awareness of Time. Welcome to the Alphas.

THE ENERGY FORMULA -053
BY Dr. BAK NGUYEN

THE ENERGY FORMULA is a book dedicated to help each individual to find the means to reach their purpose and goal in Life. Dr. Bak is a philosopher, a strategist, a business, an artist, and a dentist, how does he do all of that? He is doing so while mentoring proteges and leading the modernization of an entire industry. Until now, Momentum and Speed were the powers that he was building on and from. But those powers come from somewhere too. From a guide of our Quest of Identity, he became an ally in everyone's journey for happiness. THE ENERGY FORMULA is the book revealing step by step, the logic of building the right mindset and the way to ABUNDANCE and HAPPINESS, universally. It is not just a HOW TO book, but one that will change your life and guide you to the path of ABUNDANCE.

THE MODERN WOMAN -070
TO HAVE IT HAVE WITH NO SACRIFICE
BY Dr. BAK NGUYEN & Dr. EMILY LETRAN

In THE MODERN WOMAN: TO HAVE IT ALL WITH NO SACRIFICE, Dr. Bak joins forces with Dr. Emily Letran to empower all women to fulfill their desires, goals, and ambition. Both overachievers going against the odds, they are sharing their experience and wisdom to help all women to find confidence and support to redefine their lives. Dr. Emily Letran is a doctor in dentistry, an entrepreneur, author, and CERTIFIED HIGH-PERFORMANCE coach. For an Asian woman, she made it through the norms and the red tapes to find her voice. As she learned and grew with mentors, today she is sharing her secret with the energy that will motivate all of the female genders to stand for what they deserve. Alpha doctor, Bak is joining his voice and perspective since this is not about gender equality, but about personal empowerment and the quest of Identity of each, man and woman. Once more, Dr. Bak is bringing LEVERAGE and REASON to the new social deal between man and woman. This is not about gender, but about confidence.

THE POWER BEHIND THE ALPHA -008
BY TRANIE VO & Dr. BAK NGUYEN

It's been said by a "great man" that "We are born alone and we die alone." Both men and women proudly repeat those words as wisdom since. I apologize in advance, but what a fat LIE! That's what I learned and discovered in life since my mind and heart got liberated from the burden of scars and the ladders of society. I can have it all, not all at the same time, but I can have everything I put my mind and heart into. Actually, it is not completely true. I can have most of what I and Tranie put our minds into. Together, when we feel like one, there isn't much out of our reach. If I'm the mind, she's the heart; if I'm the Will, she's the means. Synergy is the core of our power. Tranie's aim is always Happiness. In Tranie's definition of life, there are no justifications, no excuses, no tomorrow. For Tranie, Happiness is measured by the minutes of every single day. This is why she's so strong and can heal people around her. That may also be why she doesn't need to talk much, since talking about the past or the future is, in her mind, dimming down the magic of the present, the Now. We both respect and appreciate that we are the whole balancing each other's equation of life, of love, of success. I was the plus and the minus, then I became the multiplication factor and grew into the exponential. And how is Tranie evolving in all of this? She is and always will be the balance. If anything, she is the equal sign of each equation.

THE POWER OF Dr. -066
THE MODERN TITLE OF NOBILITY
BY Dr. BAK NGUYEN, Dr. PAVEL KRASTEV AND COLLABORATORS

In THE POWER OF Dr., independent thinkers mean to exchange ideas. An idea can be very powerful if supported with a great work ethic. Work ethic, isn't that the main fabric of our white coats, scrubs, and title? In an era post-COVID where everything has been rebooted and that the healthcare industry is facing its own fate: to evolve or to be replaced, Dr. Bak and Dr. Pavel reveal the source of their power and their playbook to move forward, ahead. The power we all hold is our resilience and discipline. We put that for years at the service of our profession, from a surgical perspective. Now, we can harness that same power to rewrite the rules, the industry, and our future. Post-COVID, the rules are being rewritten, will you be part of the team or left behind?
"You can be in control!" More than personal growth and a motivational book, THE POWER OF Dr. is an awakening call to the doctor you look at when you graduate, with hope, with honour, with determination.

THE POWER OF YES -010
VOLUME ONE: IMPACT
BY Dr. BAK NGUYEN

In THE POWER OF YES, Dr. Bak is sharing his journey opening up and embracing the world, one day at a time, one ask at a time, one wish at a time. Far from a dare, saying YES allowed Dr. Bak to rewrite his mindsets and to break all the boundaries. This book is not one written a few days or weeks, but the accumulation of a journey for 12 months. The journeys started as Dr. Bak said YES to his producer to go on stage and to speak... That YES opened a world of possibilities. Dr. Bak embraced each and every one of them. 12 months later, he is celebrating the new world record of writing 9 books written over a period of 12 months. To him, it will be a miss, missing the 12 on 12 mark. To the rest of the world, they just saw the birth of a force of nature, the Alpha force. THE POWER OF YES is comprised of all the introduction of the adult books written by Dr. Bak within the first 12 months. Chapter by chapter, you can walk in his footstep seeing and smelling what he has. This is reality literature with a twist of POWER. THE POWER OF YES! Discover your potential and your power. This is the POWER OF YES, volume one. Welcome to the Alphas.

THE POWER OF YES 2 -037
VOLUME TWO: SHAPELESS
BY Dr. BAK NGUYEN

In THE POWER OF YES, volume 2, Dr. Bak is continuing his journey discovering his powers and influence. After 12 months embracing the world saying YES, he rose as an emerging force: he's been recognized as an INDUSTRIES DISRUPTOR, got nominated ERNST AND YOUNG ENTREPRENEUR OF THE YEAR, wrote 9 books within 12 months while launching the most ambitious private endeavour to reform his own industry, the dental field. Contender too many WORLD RECORDS, Dr. Bak is doing all of that in parallel. And yes, he is sleeping his nights and yes, he is writing his book himself, from the screen of his iPhone! Far from satisfied, Dr. Bak missed the mark of writing 12 books within 12 months and everything else is shaping and moving, and could come crumbling down at each turn. Now that Dr. Bak understands his powers, he is looking to test them and to push them to their limits, looking to keep scoring world records while materializing his vision and enterprises. This is the awakening of a Force of Nature looking to change the world for the better while having fun sharing. Welcome to the Alphas.

THE POWER OF YES 3 -046
VOLUME THREE: LIMITLESS
BY Dr. BAK NGUYEN

In THE POWER OF YES, volume 3, the journey of Dr. Bak continues where the last volume left, in front of 300 plus people showing up to his first solo event, a Dr. Bak's event. On stage and in this book, Dr. Bak reveals how 12 months saying YES to everything changed his life... actually, it was 18 months.
From a dentist looking to change the world from a dental chair into a multiple times world record author, the journey of openness is a rendez-vous with Fate. Dr. Bak is sharing almost in real-time his journey, experiences, but above all, his feelings, doubts, and comebacks. From one book to the next, from one journey to the next, follow the adventure of a man looking to find his name, his worth, and his place in the world. Doing so, he is touching people Doing so, he is touching people and initiating their rises. Are you ready for more? Are you ready to meet your Fate and Destiny? Welcome to the Alphas.

THE POWER OF YES 4 -087
VOLUME FOUR: PURPOSE
BY Dr. BAK NGUYEN

In THE POWER OF YES, volume 4, the journey continues days after where the last volume left. After setting the new world record of writing 48 books within 24 months, Dr. Bak is not ready to stop. As volume one covers 12 months of journey, volume 2 covers 6 months. Well, volume 3 covers 4 months. The speed is building up and increasing, steadily. This is volume 4, RISING, after breaking the sound barrier. Dr. Bak has reached a state where he is above most resistance and friction, he is now in a universe of his own, discovering his powers as he walks his journeys. This is no fiction story or wishful thinking, THE POWER OF YES is the journey of Dr. Bak, from one world record to the next, from one book to the next. You too can walk your own legend, you just need to listen to your innersole and to open up to the opportunity. May you get inspiration from the legendary journey of Dr. Bak and find your own Destiny. Welcome to the Alphas.

THE RISE OF THE UNICORN -038
BY Dr. BAK NGUYEN & Dr. JEAN DE SERRES

In THE RISE OF THE UNICORN, Dr. Bak is joining forces with his friend and mentor, Dr. Jean De Serres. Together both men had many achievements in their respective industries, but the advent of eHappyPedia, THE RISE OF THE UNICORN is a personal project dear to both of them: the QUEST OF HAPPINESS and its empowerment. This book is a special one since you are witnessing the conversation between two entrepreneurs looking to change the world by building unique tools and media. Just like any enterprise, the ride is never a smooth one in the park on a beautiful day. But this is about eHappyPedia, it is about happiness, right? So it will happen and with a smile attached to it! The unique value of this book is that you are sharing the ups and downs of the launch of a Unicorn, not just the glory of the fame, but also the doubts and challenges on the way. May it inspire you on your own journey to success and happiness.

THE RISE OF THE UNICORN 2 -076
eHappyPedia

BY Dr. BAK NGUYEN & Dr. JEAN DE SERRES

This is 2 years after starting the first tome. Dr. Bak's brand is picking up, between the accumulation of records and the recognition. eHappyPedia is now hot for a comeback. In THE RISE OF THE UNICORN 2, Dr. Bak is retracing and addressing each of Dr. Jean De Serres' concerns about the weakness of the first version of eHappyPedia and the eHappy movement. This is the sort of the creation and a UNICORN both in finance and in psychology. Never before, you will assist in such daily and decision-making process of a world phenomenon and of a company. Dr. Bak and Dr. De Serres are literally using the process of writing this series of books to plan and to brainstorm the birth of a bluechip. More than an intriguing story, this is the journey of 2 experienced entrepreneurs changing the world.

THE U.A.X STORY -072
THE ULTIMATE AUDIO EXPERIENCE

BY Dr. BAK NGUYEN

This is the story of the ULTIMATE AUDIO EXPERIENCE, U.A.X. Follow Dr. Bak's footstep on how he invented a new way to read and to learn. Dr. Bak brings his experience as a movie producer and a director to elevate the reading experience to another level with entertaining value and make it accessible to everyone, auditive, and visual people alike.

Three years plus of research and development, countless hours of trials and errors, Dr. Bak finally solved his puzzle: having written more than 1.1 million words. The irony is that he does not like to read, he likes audiobooks! U.A.X. finally allowed the opening of Dr. Bak's entire library to a new genre and media. U.A.X. is the new way to learn and enjoy Audiobooks. Made to be entertaining while keeping the self-educational value of a book, U.A.X. will appeal to both auditive and visual people. U.A.X. is the blockbuster of the Audiobooks. The format has already been approved by iTunes, Amazon, Spotify, and all major platforms for global distribution and streaming.

TIMING - TIME MANAGEMENT ON STEROIDS -074

BY Dr. BAK NGUYEN & WILLIAM BAK

In TIMING, TIME MANAGEMENT ON STEROIDS, Dr. Bak is sharing his secret to keep overachieving, overdelivering while raising the bar higher and higher. We all have 24 hours in a day, so how can some do so much more than others. Dr. Bak is not only sharing his secrets and mindset about time and efficiency, he is literally living his own words as this book is written within his last sprint to set the next world record of writing 100 books within 4 years, with only 31 days to go. With 8 books to write in 31 days, that's a little less than 4 days per book! Share the journey of a man surfing the change and looking to see where is the limit of the human mind, writing. In the meantime, understand his leverage, mindset, and secrets to challenge your own limits and dreams.

THE VACCINE -077

BY Dr. BAK NGUYEN & WILLIAM BAK

In THE VACCINE, A TALE OF SPIES AND ALIENS, Dr. Bak reprise his role as mentor to William, his 10 years-old son, both as co-author and as doctor. William is living through the COVID war and has accumulated many, many questions. That morning, they got out all at once. From a conversation between father and son, Dr. Bak is making science into words keeping the interest of his son a Saturday morning in bed. William is not just an audience, he is responsible to map the field with his questions. What started as a morning conversation between father and son, became within the next hour, a great project, their 23rd book together. Learn about the virus, vaccination while entertaining your kids.

TO OVERACHIEVE EVERYTHING BEING LAZY -090
CHEAT YOUR WAY TO SUCCESS
BY Dr. BAK NGUYEN

In TO OVERACHIEVE EVERYTHING BEING LAZY, Dr. Bak retaking his role talking to the millennials, the next generation. If in the first tome of the series LAZY, Dr. Bak addresses the general audience of millennials, especially young women, he is dedicating this tome to the ALPHA amongst the millennials, those aiming for the moon and looking, not only to be happy but to change the world. This is not another take on how to cheat your way to success or how to leverage laziness, but this is the recipe to build overachievers and rainmakers. For the young leaders with ambitions and talent, understanding TIME and ENERGY are crucial from your first steps writing your our legend. If Dr. Bak had the chance to do it all over again, this is how he would do it! Welcome to the Alphas.

TORNADO -067
FORCE OF CHANGE
BY Dr. BAK NGUYEN

In TORNADO - FORCE OF CHANGE Dr. Bak is writing solo. In the midst of the COVID war, change is not a good intention anymore. Change, constant change has become a new reality, a new norm. From somebody who holds the title of Industries' Disruptor, how does he yield change to stay in control? Well, the changes from the COVID war are constant fear and much loss of individual liberty. Some can endure the change, some will ride it. Dr. Bak is sharing his angle of navigating the changes, yielding the improvisations, and to reinvent the goals, the means to stay relevant. From fighting to keep his companies Dr. Bak went on to let go the uncontrollable to embrace the opportunity, he reinvented himself to ride the change and create opportunities from an unprecedented crisis. This is the story of a man refusing to kneel and accept defeat, smiling back at faith to find leverage and hope.

TOUCHSTONE -073
LEVERAGING TODAY'S PSYCHOLOGICAL SMOG
BY Dr. BAK NGUYEN & Dr. KEN SEROTA

TOUCHSTONE, LEVERAGING TODAY'S PSYCHOLOGICAL SMOG is mapping to navigate and to thrive in today's high and constant stress environment. After 40 years in practice, Dr. Serota is concerned about the evolution of the career of health care professionals and the never-ending level of stress. What is stress, what are its effects, damages, and symptoms? If COVID-19 revealed to the world that we are fragile, it also revealed most of the broken and the flaws of our system. For now a century, dentistry has been a champion in depression, Dr.ug addiction, and suicide rate, and the curve is far from flattening. Dr. Bak is sharing his perspective and experience dealing with stress and how to leverage it into a constructive force. From the stress of a doctor with no right to failure to the stress of an entrepreneur never knowing the future, Dr. Bak is sharing his way to use stress as leverage.

ABOUT THE AUTHOR

From Canada, **Dr BAK NGUYEN**, Nominee Ernst and Young Entrepreneur of the year, Grand Homage Lys DIVERSITY, and LinkedIn & TownHall Achiever of the year. Dr Bak is a cosmetic dentist, CEO and founder of Mdex & Co. His company is revolutionizing the dental field. Speaker and motivator, he wrote 72 books over 36 months accumulating many world records (to be officialized).

- **ENTREPRENEURSHIP**
- **LEADERSHIP**
- **QUEST OF IDENTITY**
- **DENTISTRY AND MEDICINE**
- **PARENTING**
- **CHILDREN BOOKS**
- **PHILOSOPHY**

In 2003, he founded Mdex, a dental company upon which in 2018, he launched the most ambitious private endeavour to reform the dental industry, Canada wide. Philosopher, he has close to his heart the quest of happiness of the people surrounding him, patients and colleagues alike. In 2020, he launched an International collaborative initiative named **THE ALPHAS** to share knowledge and for Entrepreneurs and Doctors to thrive through the Greatest Pandemic and Economic depression of our time.

In 2016, he co-found with Tranie Vo, Emotive World Incorporated, a tech research company to use technology to empower happiness and sharing. U.A.X. the ultimate audio experience is the landmark project on which the team is advancing, utilizing the technics of the movie industry and the advancement in ARTIFICIAL INTELLIGENCE to save the book industry and to upgrade the continuing education space.

These projects have allowed Dr Nguyen to attract interests from the international and diplomatic community and he is now the center of a global discussion in the wellbeing and the future of the health profession. It is in that matter that he shares his thoughts and encourages the health community to share their own stories.

"It's not worth it go through it alone! Together, we stand, alone, we fall."

Motivational speaker and serial entrepreneur, philosopher and author, from his own words, Dr Nguyen describes himself as a dentist by circumstances, an entrepreneur by nature and a communicator by passion.

He also holds recognitions from the Canadian Parliament and the Canadian Senate.

www.DrBakNguyen.com

UAX

ULTIMATE AUDIO EXPERIENCE

A new way to learn and enjoy Audiobooks. Made to be entertaining while keeping the self-educational value of a book, UAX will appeal to both auditive and visual people. UAX is the blockbuster of the Audiobooks.

UAX will cover most of Dr Bak's books, and is now negotiating to bring more authors and more titles to the UAX concept. Now streaming on Spotify, Apple Music and available for download on all major music platforms. Give it a try today!

AMAZON - BARNES & NOBLE - APPLE BOOKS - KINDLE
SPOTIFY - APPLE MUSIC

FROM THE SAME AUTHOR
Dr Bak Nguyen

www.DrBakNguyen.com

CHILDREN'S BOOK
with William Bak

The Trilogy of Legends

THE SPIES AND ALIENS COLLECTION

THE POWER OF YES 3
VOLUME THREE: LIMITLESS
BY Dr BAK NGUYEN

046 -

087 - **THE POWER OF YES 4**
VOLUME FOUR: PURPOSE
BY Dr BAK NGUYEN

THE POWER OF YES - 010
VOLUME ONE: IMPACT
BY Dr BAK NGUYEN

091 - **THE POWER OF YES 5**
VOLUME FIVE: ALPHA
BY Dr BAK NGUYEN

THE POWER OF YES 2 - 037
VOLUME TWO: SHAPELESS
BY Dr BAK NGUYEN

092 - **THE POWER OF YES 6**
VOLUME SIX: PERSPECTIVE
BY Dr BAK NGUYEN

www.DrBakNguyen.com

AMAZON - BARNES & NOBLE - APPLE BOOKS - KINDLE
SPOTIFY - APPLE MUSIC

DR.

Bak Nguyen

www.ingramcontent.com/pod-product-compliance
Lightning Source LLC
Chambersburg PA
CBHW060750050426

42449CB00008B/1347